Fearon Teacher Aids, Carthage, Illinois

YOU ARE THE EDITOR

61 EDITING LESSONS THAT IMPROVE WRITING SKILLS

Eric Johnson

5TH GRADE AND UP

MAKEMASTER® Blackline Masters

We thank four very experienced classroom teachers and their students for their invaluable help in making this book workable and practical. The teachers are Harrington Bell, Drexel Hill Junior High School; Dorothy J. Fread, Ada Lewis Middle School; Catherine Hineline, Germantown Friends School; and Florence Rock, Philadelphia High School for the Creative and Performing Arts.

Cover and interior designer: Ruth Scott
Calligrapher: Gustavo Medina
Interior illustrator: Jim M'Guinness
Cover illustrator: Duane Bibby

ISBN—0–8224–7696–7

Printed in the United States of America.

1.9 8

CONTENTS

CONTENTS continued

EDIT ORGANIZATION, ORDER, TRANSITIONS, CLARITY

EDIT STYLE, TONE, SUBJECTS

INTRODUCTION FOR THE TEACHER: WHY AND HOW TO USE THIS BOOK

A BASIC PROBLEM

All over America people are saying, "Today's students can't write." It's true that too many students want merely to avoid making mistakes when they write rather than to say something; other students write quite freely but are inexcusably careless (or ignorant) about errors and the clear expression of ideas. It's true also that with large classes and the press of other work, many teachers don't find the time to assign much writing and don't deal adequately with the writing they are able to assign. Parents, teachers, and even students cry for help. *You Are the Editor* is designed to provide help—in a new way.

A SOLUTION TO THE PROBLEM

The operating assumption underlying this book is that if students can learn to be editors of their own writing, before and after turning it in, much of the writing problem will be solved. Editors are people who recognize that writing is a process during which most writers sometimes make mistakes in mechanics, set down ideas in a confused way, and write inappropriately for their readers and for their own purposes. Many writers find it hard to get started, to get stopped, to keep going in the middle. Often they need to rethink, reorganize, reexpress, cut, develop, clarify, and correct. Editors help solve these problems, and when students learn from this book how to edit, they will be learning how to improve their own writing—by editing it. They will be alert to errors but not paralyzed by the fear of making them. They will recognize problems of content, interest, organization, tone, and form, and will be encouraged by knowing how to go about solving those problems.

And you, the teacher, will be blessed too. Much of the responsibility for correcting and improving (that is, editing) writing will be shifted from you to your students. Papers will be edited in advance by the writers themselves.

THE PLAN OF THIS BOOK

How are all these marvels to be wrought? Here is the scheme:

o The first three lessons in this book have students take an editor's look, in retrospect, at the writing they have done and, in the process, get some idea of what editing and self-editing can do for them.

o Next come eleven lessons that teach students fourteen editor's marks:

and how to use them. These lessons are followed by two test reviews.

o The next eight lessons require the use of editor's marks mainly on spelling problems. In editing spelling, students review fundamental spelling rules and some pesky spelling demons.

o The thirteen lessons that follow have students edit passages containing problems in punctuation, capitalization, and grammar, with one additional lesson to serve as a review and test.

o Editing for organization, order, transitions, and clarity constitutes the next eight lessons.

o Student editors consider problems of style, tone, interest, developing, cutting, and topic selection in the next thirteen lessons, which are followed by a lesson on proofreading and a review/test lesson on editing for style.

o Then, there are two editing tests. One tests knowledge of editor's marks and the other tests skill in editing a long passage. When students pass these tests, they qualify for the Editor's Certificate (page 90).

o The final section of student material is the "Writer/Editor's Handbook." This handbook includes self-editor's checklists; a display of editor's marks; some basic rules of capitalization, spelling, and punctuation; starter ideas; and other material helpful to student writers and editors. After editor's marks have been mastered, the handbook pages should be duplicated, stapled or three-hole-punched for notebooks, and given to each student to keep at his or her desk to refer to.

o The last part of the book is the "Answer Key and Teacher's Notes." In many cases the lessons have no single set of correct answers. For these lessons, the answer key either will give no answers or will provide suggested answers to use as a guide for correcting papers. The notes state each lesson's purpose and offer suggestions about how to present, correct, and extend the lessons.

NEW MATERIAL AND REVIEW MATERIAL

The mechanics of editing will almost certainly be new to students. But other material in *You Are the Editor*—spelling, punctuation, capitalization, organization, and style—should be more or less familiar. The book assumes that students have studied the basic principles of grammar and composition. Lessons relating to these subjects are meant to review students' knowledge by presenting familiar material in a new way, using editing as the vehicle.

EXTENDING EDITING SKILLS

There's no point in students learning to edit their writing unless they exercise their skills after they've finished the lessons in *You Are the Editor*. You should encourage, even require, students to continue acting as self-editors. The pages in the "Writer/Editor's Handbook" are designed to promote this continuity. You may even want to make posters of some of these pages to put up in various spots around the room. A Self-Editor's Checklist—Before Beginning the Paper; Editor's Marks; A Self-Editor's Checklist—Before Handing in the Paper; and Symbols Teachers Use in Correcting Papers can all work well as posters.

One page of the "Writer/Editor's Handbook" may prove particularly valuable in helping your students understand the editing and revisions required of them. Symbols Teachers Use in Correcting Papers (page 100) shows twenty-seven common teacher-correction symbols and gives a brief description of each. Rather than having to check with you each time they can't recall what *K, s-v,* or *r-o* means, your students can look up the symbols in the handbook.

By all means, encourage students to keep using the handbook to guide them. Occasionally set aside the first few minutes of a writing period for reviewing the pages of the handbook. From time to time, you may ask to see edited first drafts before final drafts are written, and thus check the editing rather than final products. Review editor's marks from time to time, as you review the rules of grammar and composition.

However you choose to continue what *You Are the Editor* begins, the point is to continue. Keep those writers writing and editing.

IN WHAT GRADES SHOULD THIS BOOK BE USED?

You Are the Editor is intended for use by students from middle-school on up. The editor's marks and their use can be learned by fifth graders; high-school students and adults will benefit from learning them too. Although the editing lessons range from easy to very difficult, within most of the lessons there is not only something for the young and limited to benefit from, but also enough to challenge the very able. In some of the lessons, such as those on editing for tone, order, word choice, and interest, there are no cut-and-dried answers; many students will find these lessons particularly challenging.

All students should be able to do Lessons 1–38. These lessons involve the mechanics of editing (editor's marks) and the mechanics of writing (spelling, capitalization, punctuation). Lessons 39–61 involve more sophisticated material on organization and style. They may be too complicated and difficult for less able students but can be used selectively with more advanced students.

You know and can best judge your students and their abilities. Study the lessons carefully yourself, and then decide which ones are appropriate for your entire class and which would work well only for particular students.

Each lesson is self-explanatory, and most students will be able to do the lessons without your help. The "Answer Key and Teacher's Notes" (pages 101–140) does provide suggestions for using each lesson, however, as well as answers to the lessons where applicable. Before presenting a lesson, it might serve you best to study that lesson yourself and read the notes in the "Answer Key and Teacher's Notes."

If the entire class is doing a lesson together, it can be helpful—though it is not necessary—to read and discuss the directions, *Hints,* and examples with them. Then students edit the assignment provided. Those who finish early can start work on the *Extra* activity provided at the end of each lesson. When most have finished the basic lesson, there are several ways to correct it. Which method is best depends largely on the content of the lesson. Use the answer key to suggest different editing possibilities. The methods are:

o Dictate answers to the whole class, with students correcting their own papers. Write and demonstrate difficult points on the chalkboard.

o Divide the class into small groups, with a moderator for each. Let the students read suggested answers around the group for discussion, referring to you when they need to (the same discussion can be done with pairs of students).

o Have several students (*very* clearly) write their editings on the chalkboard and discuss them, with other students studying and correcting their own papers at their desks.

o Collect the papers, correct them yourself, and the next day, teach a lesson on troublespots. Remember, except for several review and/or test lessons, the purpose of the exercises is to teach and to give practice in editing, not to test, and therefore the lessons should not be graded. In many of the lessons, as in any out-of-class writing situation, there are several possibilities for good editing (and vast possibilities for poor editing!). If you do collect student papers, you might label each with a +, 0, or − to indicate whether or not a serious, moderately successful effort has been made. But learning, not grading, is the point.

The lessons in *You Are the Editor* are ideal for use in classrooms involving individualized instruction. Students may "contract" to do the lessons at a certain rate or over a certain period. Lessons can be duplicated, labeled, and stored on shelves, and students can do each lesson as time permits.

The only lessons that should not be made generally available are Tests I and II (pages 85 and 86) and, if you expect to use them as tests, the review/test lessons (Lessons 15, 16, 38, and 61).

You can start with Lesson I and proceed in sequence to the last lesson. The first three lessons, "An Editor's Look at Your Own Writing," may be omitted if you'd rather use your own method of instructing students about the nature and value of editing. However, the thirteen lessons that teach and review the editor's marks, Lessons 4–16, should be assigned in fairly rapid succession, perhaps as a unit on the mechanics of editing.

After that, pick and choose freely, as the situation and needs of your students dictate. You may judge some lessons as too hard for your classes, others as too easy. And some may be inappropriate. If your class has few problems with spelling, for example, or if you have an established method for reviewing spelling, you may choose to omit Lessons 17–24. If you'd rather review punctuation, capitalization, and grammar another way, omit Lessons 25–38.

page 3

TIMING	There are sixty-one lessons in this book. Some can be done in ten to fifteen minutes (with ten to fifteen minutes more for correction or discussion). Others may take most of a class period, or more. It's safe to say that, along with other schoolwork, the lessons provide enough material for two or three months' work, although they could all be completed by a class (or by an individual student) in a month of very concentrated work. The best speed, once Lessons 4–16 on the mechanics of editing are done, is according to need. You might want to wait until the end of a punctuation unit to present the editing lessons on punctuation or to wait until the end of a composition unit to present the lessons on order, tone, and style, and so forth throughout the year.
EXTRAS	Each lesson (with the exception of review lessons) ends with an *Extra* for the fast finishers and for the ambitious. The *Extras* aren't "rewards" for finishing quickly but rather further assignments that are often quite demanding. Let students know that anyone completing an *Extra* will indeed get extra credit. Or use *Extras* as in-class or homework assignments to reinforce what the editing lessons have taught the students.
HINTS	Although the main purpose of this book is to teach self-editing as a way to improve one's own writing, a by-product is the review of the basic rules of punctuation, capitalization, and spelling, as well as principles of organization, clarity, tone, and sentence structure and flow. The *Hints* in various lessons represent a concise review of these rules and principles. For a more thorough review, students need to consult texts that address the material in detail.
A NOTE ON SPELLING	Great care has been taken to make sure that lessons requiring the editing of spelling also *reinforce correct spelling,* rather than requiring students to discriminate between correctly and incorrectly spelled words. On most pages where spelling words are to be edited, the correct spelling appears in bold-faced type, and students are always required to copy these spellings. (On some pages, where a number of different editing tasks are required, words are occasionally spelled incorrectly and the correct spelling is not given. This is *never* the case, however, in lessons focusing solely, or principally, upon spelling.)
REINFORCING EDITING SKILLS	Once your students have been introduced to the mechanics and skills of editing, you may incorporate editing into your writing program as follows:

1. Have students write first drafts of their papers.
2. Have them edit their papers, using what they've learned about editing.
3. Have them share their papers with other students for editorial comment (and even correction).
4. Have them prepare second drafts, using the feedback from step 3, and hand them in to you.
5. Read the papers, comment on them, mark them with the symbols for teacher correction (page 100), and return them to the students.
6. Have students rewrite and correct their papers as needed, and hand them back in for final checking.
7. If the papers deserve treatment as major works (such as term papers and science reports), have students do a final edit and then copy their papers in final draft, proofread that draft, and hand the papers in for final evaluation.

Note that in this way most of the work of writing and editing becomes the students' work. You have supervised the process, but students, by incorporating self-editing into the process of writing, have learned to improve their *own* writing.

Lesson 1

WHY BE THE EDITOR?

Editors help writers write better. If you learn to edit, you can help *yourself* write better. Here are fifteen ways in which editing may improve your writing. Decide how much of each kind of improvement you need. Then mark your decision in the square before each statement:

3 = great need; 2 = some need; 1 = no need.

1. ☐ to correct my spelling

2. ☐ to correct my punctuation

3. ☐ to correct my use of capital and small letters

4. ☐ to choose the best words to say what I want

5. ☐ to start writing without fear of making mistakes

6. ☐ to go back and correct mistakes made in the first writing

7. ☐ to decide how to begin my papers

8. ☐ to make my writing more interesting

9. ☐ to cut the dull places from what I've written

10. ☐ to develop the interesting parts of what I've written

11. ☐ to organize my writing clearly

12. ☐ to write good conversation (dialogue)

13. ☐ to avoid papers that are too long or too short

14. ☐ to stop being afraid of words that are hard to spell

15. ☐ to invent good ideas to write about

16. ☐ other: _____

EXTRA Look over and think about what you have just done. Then write a convincing paragraph on the subject: *How Learning to Edit Can Help Me Write Better.*

Lesson 2

HERE'S MY BEST!

Look over, or think over, all the writing you have done. Choose one of the best pieces of writing you have ever done. It doesn't matter whether you still have the paper or merely remember it. It doesn't matter why you wrote it or for whom. Neither does it matter whether you wrote it in school or out of school. Answer the following questions about that piece of writing.

1. What was the subject or title? _____
_____

2. Approximately when was it written? _____

3. For whom did you write it? _____
_____

4. Why did you write it? _____
_____

5. Write a brief summary of what was in it. _____
_____
_____
_____

6. What do you think was especially good about it? _____
_____
_____
_____

7. How do you know it was good? _____
_____
_____
_____

Extra Think of a story or book you've read that you liked very much. On another piece of paper, write the title of the story or book and the name of the author. Then answer questions 5, 6, and 7 about it.

Lesson 3

HERE'S MY WORST!

Even the best writers sometimes write badly. Think over your past writing and choose a paper that really flopped. It can be an in-school paper or an out-of-school paper. It doesn't matter if you no longer have it. In fact, you were probably very happy to throw it away. Answer the following questions about that piece of bad writing.

1. What was the subject or title? _____
   _____

2. Approximately when was it written? _____

3. For whom did you write it? _____
   _____

4. Why did you write it? _____
   _____
   _____

5. Write a very brief summary of what was in it. _____
   _____
   _____
   _____

6. What do you think was especially bad about it? _____
   _____
   _____
   _____

7. How do you know it was bad? _____
   _____
   _____
   _____

EXTRA Think of a story or book you've read that you didn't like. On another piece of paper, write the title of the story or book and the name of the author. Then answer questions 5, 6, and 7 about it.

Lesson 4

DELETE AND CLOSE THE GAP

When you write you sometimes put in letters that should not be there. Editors remove such mistakes by using the *delete* mark (shown at the right). It means "take out" or "delete":

The boy spat on on the floor floor.

Another mark editors use is the *close* mark (shown at the right). It means "close," and it closes a gap that shouldn't be there:

My bed room is some times so crowwded

that I musst sleep on the car pet.

When a letter is deleted from inside a word, it leaves a gap to be closed:

crowwded sleep deelete closse

Using delete and close marks, edit the following passage.

Suppose I some how got to to be an editor. I woulld eddit my littlel brother and and sisster out off my bed room. There would n't bee anny gapps to cloase. In stead, I'd yuse two deelete mmarks, and thatt woulld bee all! Off course, Momm and Dadd meight nott nott like it, but I coulld jusst jusst say, "Keepp them in side youre youre roome." I'de even even pay them fieve dollarrs a a day for the ser vice, un till I ended up inn thee thee poor house. May be I'd like it therre.

Some correct spellings: **bedroom, close, dollars, instead, might, poorhouse, somehow, until, wouldn't**

Extra Write a paragraph that needs lots of delete and close marks. Give it to a classmate to edit. Write very clearly.

YOU ARE THE EDITOR © COPYRIGHT

Lesson 5

KEEP IT IN   *stet* _ _ _ _ _

Sometimes writers or editors take something out (delete), then decide they want to keep it in after all. Here's how they mark what is to be kept:

stet /

My mother was ~~rather~~ angry at me.

The *stet* in the margin is the Latin word for "stay." The broken line under the letters shows what is supposed to stay in.

Edit the following paragraph for stets. Use one stet in the margin next to each line for each word or group of words you think should stay. For some lines you'll need more than one stet. And in some cases, you may choose not to stet what is deleted.

I'm not ~~certain~~ sure why we have so many ~~lots of~~ insects around our house. But I've got ~~a few~~ ideas. It could be because my sister's room is ~~even~~ dirtier than my brother's.   Even my parents are not ~~not~~ a miracle of ~~complete~~ cleanliness.   They've been known to leave our sink ~~very~~ full of dirty dishes for many days~~, and days~~.   Anyway,   insects' appetites are ~~surprisingly~~ strong, and they'll march to wherever ~~all~~ food and dirt are ~~lying~~ lying around. You might call it "the bugs' hunger journey ~~or trip~~."   After ~~all~~, bugs have to ~~eat~~ too.   And there is plenty ~~enough~~ for them to eat around our house.

Extra Write some sentences or a paragraph that need "keep it in" marks. Give your paper to a classmate to edit.

ADD SOMETHING

Writers sometimes leave out necessary letters or words. Editors add what's needed by using a *caret* mark shown at the right:

$\wedge$

som*l*thing; ban*a*na; Because of mistakes I failed *the* test.

The following passage contains nearly thirty words with a letter or letters omitted and about twenty-five places where a word is missing. Edit the passage using carets to show where to put the needed additions.

Som peple say that girls diferent from boy. They that girl are gentl and nice, but every boy tough and rude. Wel, maybe that what peple saying, but everybody I know doesn't fit with people say. My friend's sistr, example, whose name Sally, is extreme strong fierce. She able beat up boy who are whole year oldr than she is, and she not at all gentle nice. Howevr, does get very marks in scool, and the all like her as pupil. On other hand, own bother, a boy year older than I, is alway read books and gentl and nice except he's mad. Then he laugh very and stamp out of room. Anywa, my ida is that you can't make genral statments girls and boy. You have ask: "Wich girl? Wich boy?"

Some correct spellings: **different, everybody, general, gentle, idea, people, school, statements, which**

Extra Make up ten sentences with letters and words missing.
Let a classmate, using carets to make additions, edit your sentences.

CHANGE OR ADD LETTERS

You know that editors use carets to add missing letters. They also use carets to correct wrong letters in words:

g$\stackrel{i}{\wedge}$rl $\stackrel{c}{\wedge}$at stud$\stackrel{y}{\wedge}$ing

Sometimes words have both missing letters and wrong letters. Practice using this editing tool on some spelling demons. First be sure you know the correct spelling of the words. Study the list at the bottom of the page. Now edit the misspelled words below. After editing each word, write it correctly in the blank following it.

alreddy	_____	excelant	_____
amung	_____	expiriance	_____
ansser	_____	familar	_____
argement	_____	imbarrassed	_____
busyness	_____	inneresting	_____
captin	_____	libary	_____
coler	_____	opinnon	_____
cumpletly	_____	probally	_____
deside	_____	relize	_____
develup	_____	seperate	_____
diferant	_____	suprize	_____
docter	_____	ussally	_____

Some correct spellings: **already, among, answer, argument, business, captain, color, completely, decide, develop, different, doctor, embarrassed, excellent, experience, familiar, interesting, library, opinion, probably, realize, separate, surprise, usually**

Extra Write some sentences or a paragraph using all of the above twenty-four words in a way that makes sense. Underline each of the twenty-four words. Try to spell them correctly but, just in case, give them to a classmate to edit.

ADD SPACE

Youmayknowthatsomepeoplemakecareless

mistakesandrunwordstogether.

Tocorrectthis, editors use the *space* mark (shown at the right). It means "space needed here." # #

#

You|may|know ...

Now correct the sentence above, using twelve space marks.

Below is a fable written by a strange person who forgot to leave spaces. To edit it you'll need nearly 140 space marks. Be sure to show a space after each comma and period.

Onherheadacountrygirlwascarryingapailofmilkto

markettosell.Asshewalkedalong,shesangamerrysongand

busilythoughtaboutwhatwonderfulthingsshewoulddo

withthemoneyshewouldget.Shewouldbuyagoodhen,and

thelovelyhenwouldlaybeautifuleggs.Theeggswouldhatch

intohealthylittlechicksthatwouldgrowupintonicefatbirds

thatthegirlwouldsell.Shewouldusethemoneytostartsaving

togotoveterinaryschool.Thenshewouldbeabletocurethe

diseasesofallthefarmanimalsandwouldbeveryusefultothe

farmers.Thethoughtmadeherlaughoutloudwithpleasure.

Shelaughedsohardthatherheadshookandherbodyrocked,

andshespilledeverydropofmilk.Themoralis:Don'tcount

yourchickensbeforetheyarehatched.

EXTRA Write a brief story. Run all the words together as in the fable above. Give it to a classmate to edit with space marks. Write or print each letter *very* clearly.

Lesson 9

SWITCH THEM

Obviousyl, this snetence si in veyr bda

rtouble. Do yuo see hwy?

An editor uses the *transpose* mark (shown at the right) to reverse the order of letters or words. *Transpose* means "switch positions," and the mark works like this:

Obviousyl, this snetence ...

Now correct the sentence above. You'll need eight transpose marks.

Editors also use transpose marks to change the order of words:

my cat big

Use four transpose marks to correct this sentence:

Now me tell, what did rug the say the to

floor? I've you got covered!

Be the editor and correct the following passages. You will need more than forty transpose marks.

After you edit, write (on a separate sheet) the correct spelling of all the words that had reversed letters.

1. Sign a in calssroom: It is safe make to a mitsake in

thsi lcassroom, btu is it better much fro you make to a

differetn one time each. Then are you learnnig.

2. A third-grader was aksed why she not did watn

go to bakc to school. She repiled, "I can't read, I

wriet can't, and won't thye me let talk."

3. Definition homework of: A thnig kids don't any have

of wehn it's tiem for favorite their VT progarm, btu

have they great piles of wehn time it's to go bed to.

4. Riddle: Waht elephanst do have that other no

animlas have? Answer: elephants baby

Extra
Write some short paragraphs containing reversed letters and words. Write very clearly. Give them to a classmate to edit.

YOU ARE THE EDITOR COPYRIGHT © 1981

Lesson 10

PAUSE AND STOP

Editors show that a comma is needed by using the *comma* mark (shown at the right). They show that a period is needed by using the *period* mark (shown just below the comma mark). Here is a sentence with commas and a period added:

Please౯ John౯ pass the bread☉

These special marks make the corrections very easy to see.

In the following passages, all the commas and periods have been omitted. You will need nineteen comma marks and seventeen period marks to correct them.

HINT 1: Most of the time, commas are used to mark pauses.   HINT 2: Periods mark the ends of sentences and abbreviations.

1. Our teacher Mr J R Firmly came into the room   He looked straight at Molly and said "Molly your hands are filthy   What would you say if I came to class with dirty hands like that?"

   "Well " said Molly   "I think Mr Firmly I'd be too polite to mention it "

2. Mrs Mary R Jones is a Scout den mother   One day her Cub Scouts were late for their meeting

   "Boys you are late " she said   "Please Jimmy explain why "

   "Well " said Jimmy "we were helping an old man cross the street "

   "Very nice " said Mrs Jones "but that doesn't take half an hour does it?"

   "Well " said Jimmy "we had trouble   He didn't want to go "

Extra
Write some passages with commas and periods missing and give them to a classmate to edit. Tell your classmate how many commas and periods you think there should be.

Lesson 11

ADD APOSTROPHES ˅

When an apostrophe is left out, editors add it this way:

˅
youve

Edit the paragraph below for missing apostrophes.

HINT 1: Apostrophes show what belongs to what or to whom (*the cat's meow, the girls' gym, Mr. Jones's hat, the men's umbrellas*). ✍ **HINT 2:** Apostrophes in contractions show where letters have been left out (*she's—she is; can't—cannot; you'll—you will; they're—they are*).

Ill tell you this, today Im very happy. I dont know why, exactly. But I think its because of my teacher. You see, shes teaching me how to edit. Youre probably wondering why that makes me happy. Heres the reason: I love to write, but my writings very sloppy, like my brothers room. Ive got great ideas, but theyre usually lost among all my mistakes.

My teachers always saying, "A persons writing must be clear." Shes right. It doesnt help to have great ideas if people cant understand them.

My teacher also says, "Editings a writers helper." Shes right about that too. And in the same way my brothers room needs a janitor, my writing needs an editor. Since Im learning to edit, Ill be the editor !

Extra Write a paragraph using lots of words that need apostrophes, but leave the apostrophes out. Give the paragraph to a classmate to edit.

Lesson 12

CAPITAL AND SMALL LETTERS ≡ /

This is how editors show that a small letter should be capitalized:

n̲ebraska

This is how they show that a capital letter should be written small:

C̸andy

Here's an edited sentence:

m̲y S̸ister a̲my hates W̸inter,

B̸ut she L̸oves j̲im.

Now edit the passages below for mistakes in capitalization.

HINT 1: Capitalize the first word of a sentence, proper names *(Dallas, Ken)* and proper adjectives *(French, American)*, and the names of days, months, and organizations *(Monday, May, the American Red Cross)*. ✍ **HINT 2:** Don't capitalize seasons *(spring, fall)*, or words such as *uncle* or *mother* unless they are part of a name *(Uncle Ben)*.

1. the tv Announcer said: "you've heard both our Editorial And a Reply to our Editorial. now Here is jane castle, speaking for Those who have No Opinion."

2. he went to california to get into the Movies and He did get In. He Sells Popcorn at a Drive-In.

3. a long-Winded preacher came to Church with a Bandaged Finger. He explained, "you see, I was Thinking about my Sermon and cut my Finger."

after the sermon, a Member said to Him, "perhaps it Would have been Better, reverend jackson, to Think about your Finger and cut Your Sermon."

4. "i hate Wars," Said the Child. "they make too much History."

EXTRA Make up some passages that contain mistakes in capitalization and give them to a classmate to edit.

PARAGRAPHS AND QUOTATION MARKS

Usually, a new paragraph starts when writing shifts from one main idea to another. Editors show that a new paragraph is needed by inserting the *paragraph mark* (shown at the right).

¶

In dialogue (conversation), a new paragraph starts each time a new speaker is quoted:

"You <u>love</u> spinach, Lolly," said Mom.¶"Yes,"

said Lolly, "but not enough to eat it."

Also in dialogue, the words people say are enclosed in quotation marks:

"Come on," yelled Sal, "let's get out of here!"

Editors supply omitted quotation marks by using the *quotation marks* (shown at the right).

" "

ᵛMy mother isn't here,ᵛ Jones said.

Below is a little story that hasn't been divided into paragraphs. Remember to use the paragraph mark when the main idea shifts or when a new speaker is quoted. If speech is quoted within a paragraph about the speaker, do not start a new paragraph. Also, all the quotation marks have been left out. Edit the story.

Billy was a very spoiled little boy. He refused to eat
his food. I won't! I won't! he yelled. You have to
or you'll get sick, said his mother. No, yelled
Billy, I won't! and he threw the dish across the
room. Then his father said to his mother, Let me
deal with him. All right, sighed the mother, you can
have him. Billy, said his father, you have to eat
something or you'll starve. So what do you want? I
promise I'll get it for you. Billy smiled wickedly. I
want an earthworm, he said. The father gulped but
replied, OK, a promise is a promise, and he dug up a
worm and put it on Billy's plate. I don't want it!

☞

CONTINUED

yelled Billy.   That's not the way I like worms!   I like them fried.   OK, sighed the father, and he fried the worm in butter and presented it to Billy.   It's fried and looks nice, said Billy, but maybe it's poison.   Dad, you eat half of it first.   All right, Billy, the father snarled, and he cut the worm in half, closed his eyes, and swallowed one half.   Oh, no!   wailed Billy.   I won't eat it.   Dad, look what you've done!   What's the matter <u>now</u>?   moaned the father.   Billy shouted, You ate <u>my</u> half!

Extra
Write a piece of conversation, either one you've heard or one you make up. Omit all paragraphs and quotations marks. Be sure, though, that the words make it clear who's speaking. Then give your paper to a classmate to edit.

Lesson 14

NO NEW PARAGRAPH—RUN IN

Sometimes writers start new paragraphs where they shouldn't. Editors use a *run-in* mark (shown at the right) to indicate that no new paragraph should begin. For example:

Please learn to edit. Editing your writing

gives you courage.

It helps you to write freely and then later to

improve and correct.

Edit the following passage. It needs three run-in marks. There are also nearly twenty other places where editor's marks you've already learned are needed. Add them, too.

A problem in our school is littering.

People seem to be too weak to carry papers and

trash to the nearest wastebasket.   Instead, theyre

always dropping on the floor of the halls and

classrooms classrooms, and the place rapidly become a

mess.   Its really disgusting.

One day, two of my friends and I decide to try and

experiment to people teach to stop littering we took a

sheet wrinkled of paper and taped a dollar bill on to it.

We wrote a message Right beside the bill

saying, "Congratulations!   Youve just done a good

deed by picking up this Piece of litter.

This dollar is Reward.   also, you are hereby

awarded membership in the Anti-Litter club."

name:

CONTINUED

When no one was look, we placed the piece

paper, dollar down, on the floor.   Then We leaned

against wall the and waited.

Extra Finish the story in the same style and then get a classmate to edit the ending you've written.

Lesson 15

REVIEW OF EDITOR'S MARKS I

In the blank beside each editor's mark, write what the mark does. Then give an example. The first one has been done to show you how.

1. ✓   1. *delete or remove material*

Example: *dogg*

2. ◯   2. _____

Example: _____

3. ⌀   3. _____

Example: _____

4. ∧   4. _____

Example: _____

5. #   5. _____

Example: _____

6. ∪   6. _____

Example: _____

7. ⋀   7. _____

Example: _____

8. ⊙   8. _____

Example: _____

9. *l*   9. _____

Example: _____

10. *R*   10. _____

Example: _____

11. ¶   11. _____

Example: _____

CONTINUED

12. ⅋ ⅋   12. _____

Example: _____

13. ⅋   13. _____

Example: _____

14. *stet* _ _ _ _   14. _____

Example: _____

15. ⌐   15. _____

Example: _____

_____

Words you may need to spell: **apostrophe, capitalize, delete, omit, paragraph, quotation, transpose**

REVIEW OF EDITOR'S MARKS II

Here are sixteen statements. Each tells what a certain editor's mark means. After each one, draw the mark and then give an example of how it works. The first one is done to show you how.

1. Make a space. _#_ _My dog has fleas._

2. Close the gap. _____ _____

3. Add a word or letter. _____ _____

4. Run in the two lines (no new paragraph). _____ ____

   _____

   _____

5. Make the letter a capital. _____ _____

6. Change a letter. _____ _____

7. Put back the deleted material. _____ _____

8. Start a new paragraph. _____ _____

   _____

9. Add a comma. _____ _____

10. Delete the material. _____ _____

11. Make the letter small (lower case). _____ _____

12. Add quotation marks. _____ _____

13. Delete the material and close the gap. _____ _____

   _____

14. Transpose words or letters. _____ _____

15. Add a period. _____ _____

16. Add an apostrophe. _____ _____

Lesson 17

SUFFIXES ON SILENT-e WORDS

The paragraph below contains many silent-e words that end with suffixes. Use delete marks and close marks to edit them:

com̸e ing   care͜ ful

After you've edited them, list the words, spelling them correctly.

HINT 1:   Words that end with silent e drop the e before adding a suffix that begins with a vowel *(come + ing = coming; nerve + ous = nervous)*.   ✍ **HINT 2:**   Words that end in silent e keep the e when adding a suffix that begins with a consonant *(move + ment = movement; nice + ly = nicely)*.   ✍ **HINT 3:**   Words such as *noticeable* and *courageous* keep the e to show that the c and g stay soft.   ✍ **HINT 4:**   Exceptions are *truly* and *ninth* (but *ninety,* not *ninty*).

What made the lone ly boy true ly happy was write ing stories.   Most of the stories were excite ing. He like ed create ing tales about disasters—about things crashing and come ing apart.

One story was about a man drive ing care lessly down the road at nine ty miles an hour.   All of a sudden his car started smoke ing fierce ly.   The man drive ing the car immediate ly slowed down.

At sixty miles an hour the car's engine started flame ing.   At fifty, the tires explode ed, yet the drive er didn't seem nerve ous.   At thirty miles an hour the fenders and doors flew off.   At twenty, the windows popped out.   At ten, the steering wheel began come ing off.   Finally the car stopped.   The drive er was unhurt.   He sat there smile ing.

Some correct spellings: **carelessly, creating, driver, driving, exciting, exploded, fiercely, flaming, immediately, lonely, nervous, ninety, smiling, truly, writing**

EXTRA Write a paragraph of your own containing silent-e words and suffixes. Give it to a classmate to edit.

Lesson 18

WHEN TO DOUBLE FINAL CONSONANTS

Some suffixes begin with vowels, for example, *ing, ed, er.* Certain words double the final consonant when adding such suffixes *(skip, skipped).* In the passage below there are many words with suffixes added. Some are spelled correctly and some are not. Edit the ones that are misspelled. After you've edited them, list the words, spelling them correctly.

HINT 1: Double the final consonant if the word ends with a single consonant and has only one syllable *(hit, hitting),* or if the word is pronounced with the accent on the last syllable *(begin, beginning).* ✍ **HINT 2:** Don't double the final consonant if two vowels or another consonant come right before it *(fool, fooled; start, started),* or if the word is pronounced with the accent on any syllable but the last *(open, opening).*

Lots of people are joging today. I've never liked exercise myself. I've always prefered eating to sweatting.

My friend Alice was an exercise freak. She startted every day with 100 laps in the swiming pool. She ended every day by running two miles. In between she jumpped rope and lifted weights.

In the begining, Alice benefited from all her exercise. When she began she was fater than I was. Then every day she seemmed to be getting thiner and thiner. That was fine until she started offerring me advice.

"Look what's happenning to you!" she'd say. "You're so fat your buttons are poping! How about coming to the gym with me and losing some weight?"

Every time I saw her she pated my stomach. I felt like hiting her. And I wasn't the only one.

CONTINUED

Alice was criticizing all her friends.   She needded
a good spanking.

    So we all stoped talking to her.   We just ignored
her.   Pretty soon she got the point.   She startted
being nice again.   She knew she needded friendship
not just muscles.   So she's wining friends again—and
also wining races.

Some correct spellings: **beginning, benefited, coming, criticizing, eating, ended, fatter, getting, happening, hitting, ignored, jogging, jumped, lifted, liked, losing, needed, offering, patted, popping, preferred, running, seemed, spanking, started, stopped, sweating, swimming, talking, thinner, winning**

Extra Write some sentences using words that have suffixes added. Spell some of the words correctly, some incorrectly. Give the sentences to a classmate to edit.

CHANGE y TO i TO ADD es, ed, er, est

The passage below contains many words that end with y plus
a suffix. Edit the passage to correct the misspellings.

HINT 1:   Words that end with y with a consonant before it change the y to i before adding es, ed, er, est (baby, babies; pity, pitied; easy, easier, easiest).   ✍ **HINT 2:**   All words that have a vowel before the y just add s (boy, boys).

     Bob was the happyest, merryest person I ever knew.   He told the sillyest jokes and the funnyest storys.   He was friendlyer than a litter of puppys.

     Bob didn't have any enemys, though some people said he must be the crazyest man in town.   Why? Because he never worryed about anything.   He enjoied everything and always seemed satisfyed.   He plaied with babys and bought tois for all the little girls and boys.

     All Bob's friends got busyer with their dutys and didn't take time for fun.   But Bob seemed to get happyer every day.   Some people said they pityed Bob.   "Life isn't all partys!" they cryed.   But I think they envyed him, don't you?

Some correct spellings: **babies, boys, busier, craziest, cried, duties, enemies, enjoyed, envied, friendlier, funniest, happier, happiest, merriest, parties, pitied, played, puppies, satisfied, silliest, stories, toys, worried**

EXTRA Write some sentences or a paragraph using words that end in y with suffixes added. Spell some of the words correctly, some incorrectly. Give the sentences or paragraph to a classmate to edit.

Lesson 20

ADD SUFFIXES

The paragraph below contains many words that end with *y* plus a suffix. It also contains many words that end with consonants plus suffixes. Edit the paragraph to correct the misspellings. After you've edited them, list the words, spelling them correctly.

HINT 1: Words that end with *y* with a consonant before it change the *y* to *i* before adding a suffix *(beauty, beautiful).*   ✍ **HINT 2:** However, when you add *ing*, keep the *y* *(study, studying).*   ✍ **HINT 3:** Words that end with consonants don't need any changes *(cheer, cheerful).*   ✍ **HINT 4:** Never change a suffix; just add it.

I am always studiing people's problems. I can understand bashfulness and clumsyness, but I don't understand meaness. What could be sillyer or emptyer? Meaness takes all the happyness and merryment out of life. Ignoring mean people is easer than triing to be friends with them. But they are pityful, really, and we should try to be mercyful and helpful. Otherwise they will keep spreading unhappyness.

Some correct spellings: **bashfulness, clumsiness, easier, emptier, happiness, helpful, meanness, merciful, merriment, pitiful, sillier, studying, trying, unhappiness**

Extra   Write some sentences or a paragraph using words that end with *y* with suffixes added. Spell some of the words correctly, some incorrectly. Give the paper to a classmate to edit.

Lesson 21

ADD PREFIXES

Some of the prefixes in the passage below are misspelled. You are the editor. Correct the misspelled words either by crossing them out and writing above

disappeared

~~dissappeared~~

or by using editor's marks.

dis̸appeared

After you've edited them, list the words, spelling them correctly.

HINT: When you attach a prefix to a word, never change the prefix or the word. Just put them together *(mis + spell = misspell).*

Sally was antissocial. People made her unncomfortable. She misstrusted and dissliked nearly everyone. She often wished that everyone would just dissappear.

The reason for Sally's unhappy feelings was that she felt unlloved. What's more, she felt unnable to make friends. So she told and reetold herself, "Friends are unimportant."

She hated school. Whenever she mispelled a word or missread a sentence, she thought everybody was laughing at her. When she left the room, then rentered, she was sure the children had been talking about her.

One day Sally's teacher said, "Sally, this is nosense. Your imagination is overrworked. You make yourself unllovable by thinking that it's true. So reethink!"

CONTINUED

Sally's troubles were unndone by that little

talk.   She recconsidered everything.   She decided that

she had misunderstood herself and everyone else. From

then on, she was unusually friendly.

Some correct spellings: **antisocial, disappear, disliked, misread, misspelled, mistrusted, misunderstood, nonsense, overworked, reconsidered, reentered, rethink, retold, unable, uncomfortable, undone, unhappy, unimportant, unlovable, unloved, unusually**

EXTRA Write a paragraph or several short sentences using many prefix words. Misspell some of the prefix words. Give the paragraph or sentences to a classmate to edit.

SPELLING HOMONYMS CORRECTLY

The passages below contain many misspelled *homonyms*. Homonyms are words that sound the same but that have different meanings:

I <u>hear</u> with my ears.

Come <u>here</u> to me.

Here is a list of very common homonyms that editors need to be aware of:

forth (Bring it *forth* now.)
fourth (third and *fourth*)

its (in *its* place)
it's ("it is") (*It's* here.)

their (*their* gifts)
there (here and *there*)
they're ("they are") (*They're* gone.)

to (go *to* bed)
too (*too* much; me *too*)
two (one, *two*, three)

whose (*Whose* is it?)
who's ("who is") (*Who's* there?)

your (*your* eyes)
you're ("you are") (*You're* a fake.)

Edit the passages below by correcting the misspelled words. Either cross them out and write above

who's
~~whose~~

or use editor's marks.

ther*i*~~e~~

After you've edited them, list the words, spelling them correctly.

HINT: To know which homonym to use, always think what the word means in its sentence.

1. To pigs are to many to have when there both noisy.

2. "Their is entirely two much soup," said the forth person in line. Whose in charge of this restaurant and who's ideas went into its menu? Bring them fourth. Let's see their faces!"

3. Which of you're to statues do you think is better? I'd like two see whose face its modeled on.

Lesson 22

CONTINUED

4. There fourth child is hear in you're house. Please here carefully two ideas she's saying: "Whose always in their helping me with my life and its problems? It's my father and, hear and there, my friends!"

EXTRA Write some sentences using homonyms; misspell some, correctly spell others. Give your paper to a classmate to edit.

ie/ei ERRORS

The paragraph below contains twenty-nine words that are spelled with either *ei* or *ie*. Edit the paragraph by writing in the correct letters.

The boy's fr *ie* nd enjoyed l *ei* sure.

After you've edited them, list the words, spelling them correctly.

HINT 1: When sound is ee, put *i* before *e* (*field, chief, believe*) except after *c* (*receive, ceiling*).
HINT 2: When sound is not ee, put *e* before *i* (*weigh, eight, foreign*). **HINT 3:** Exceptions are: He *seized* (n)either *weird leisure*; and his *friend* did *mischief* with a *sieve*.

The n___ghbor of the f___rce cash___r is a fr___nd of mine. He had a w___rd problem with ach___vement tests. He tried work and he tried l___sure, but n___ther of them helped. Then he walked through quiet f___lds before the test. He ate a p___ce of cake, but he was gr___ved to find no rel___f from his ch___f problem. He thought of becoming a th___f or wearing a v___l like a for___gner. This might sh___ld him from his n___ce. She bel___ved that his brain was ___ther a s___ve or a counterf___t. At last he became h___ to a fr___ght car full of golden s___ves. They went from floor to c___ling. He sold these from a p___r in the harbor, got rich, and became conc___ted and misch___vous.

Some correct spellings: **achievement, believed, cashier, ceiling, chief, conceited, counterfeit, either, fields, fierce, foreigner, freight, grieved, heir, leisure, mischievous, neighbor, neither, niece, piece, pier, relief, shield, sieve, sieves, weird**

Extra
Make up an *ie/ei* exercise of your own and give it to a classmate to try.

Lesson 24

FORTY SPELLING DEMONS

The following passage contains forty words that are often misspelled. Twenty-nine of them are misspelled here. Edit the passage. Either cross out the error and correctly write the word above or use editor's marks to correct the error. After you've edited them, list the words, spelling them correctly.

In Febuary the quite doctor surprized evrybody. She gave up medicine. She'd finlly deceided to try a diffrent busyness. What could she do? The answer, she thoght, was to study grammer and be an editor. That would probly be more intresting than medacine.

She seperated herself from her freinds and spent her time amoung books. She spent hours every day in the libary, with usually only ten minits for lunch. It was definitly hard work, but it was neccesary. She studied untill her head was stuffed with opinnions.

At last she was ready. She drove across the countery looking for an exellent editing oppertunity. But she didn't suceed. She was completly dissapointed and embarrassed. Everywhere, people had become sensible and had learned to edit their own writing. Therefore, she changed jobs agen.

Forty demons: **across, again, among, answer, better, business, completely, could, country, decided, definitely, different, disappointed, doctor, embarrassed, excellent, everybody, February, finally, friend, grammar, interesting, library, meant, medicine, minute, necessary, opinion, opportunities, perhaps, probably, quiet, sensible, separate, succeed, surprise, therefore, thought, until, usually**

Extra

Select ten to twenty common words that are difficult for some people in your class to spell. Use them in a paragraph, misspelling some of them. Give the paragraph to a classmate to edit.

CORRECT PUNCTUATION
AT THE ENDS OF SENTENCES

The paragraph below contains twenty sentences. But the editor sees right away that each needs a punctuation mark at the end. You are the editor. Put in the correct punctuation marks.

for a question ?

for an exclamation !

for a statement, a request, or a command ⊙

It is often a matter of judgment whether or not to use an exclamation mark. It depends on what effect you want.

Alicia was thinking about her problems   Why was she doing so poorly in school   Why did she have troubles with writing   Oh, what a miserable life she was leading   She was dying for help with her problems   They simply had to be solved   Then she had an inspiration   Editing, yes, that would do it   Alicia started learning to edit   She learned how to use editor's marks   She even taught them to her best friends   What do you think was the result   Well, I'll tell you   They all got A's in English   How amazing that is   Therefore, students, please learn how to edit   Why not try it   You'll never regret it   It might even help people to communicate better   So, let's go

EXTRA Write a paragraph that contains question sentences, exclamation sentences, and request, statement, and command sentences. Leave out the punctuation marks at the end of each sentence. Give the paragraph to a classmate to edit.

Lesson 26

RUN-ON SENTENCES

Run-on sentences are two or more sentences that run together without a period separating them. Sometimes run-on sentences have commas separating them, instead of periods. Punctuate the sentences below so that they don't run on. Start each new sentence with a capital letter and end each one with a period. You can change a comma to a period just by putting a circle around it.

Tom went home⊙ Sally put on her skates⊙

HINT: You can usually "hear" where a sentence should end. As you read aloud, your voice usually pauses and drops in pitch at the end of a sentence. As you edit, it might help you to read the passages aloud very quietly and to listen to what your voice does.

1. the small boy promised never to lie he forgot how hard truth is

2. a skunk is a cute, cuddly animal however, the smell is not cuddly that's why skunks don't get hugged

3. never go near the edge you might fall in then you'd really be sorry

4. a teacher pinned a dollar bill under a piece of paper then he dropped it in the hall a first grader picked it up and won the No-Litter Prize

5. size is less important than brains at least that's what my friend thinks he's four feet tall and weighs fifty-one pounds

6. we think our sun is very large if it were hollow, it could contain a million earths however, there are stars in space that could contain half a billion of our suns there are 100 billion stars in an average galaxy finally, in the universe there may be 100 million galaxies

EXTRA Write some passages or a paragraph containing run-on sentences. Give your paper to a classmate to edit.

Lesson 27

SENTENCE FRAGMENTS

Below is a paragraph containing several *fragments*. Fragments are pieces of sentences punctuated as if they were complete sentences. By changing the punctuation and capitalization, edit the paragraph so that it has all complete sentences. The first four sentences are done to show you how. Three of the sentences in the paragraph are complete and don't need changing.

You won't need to add or subtract words, but you will need to use editor's marks.

HINT: Read aloud very quietly and listen for groups of words followed by periods that sound as if they need something more to complete them. Combine these groups with other words to make whole sentences.

It was raining hard. When Brian came home from school. Because he had forgotten his raincoat. He was soaked. Even worse, he was freezing cold. What he wanted more than anything else was a bowl of that good hot soup. That his mother often had ready for him. On days like this. But when he opened the door and called upstairs. There was no answer. Where was Mom? Then Brian became aware of soft laughter. Coming from the basement. He grew very scared. He was shivering not only from the cold. But also from terror. Quietly going outside again. Brian yelled for help. Hoping a good neighbor would hear him. And would come to the rescue.

Extra Write a paragraph of your own containing several sentence fragments. Give it to a classmate to edit.

Lesson 28

COMMAS

The sentences in the paragraph below have the correct punctuation marks at the ends. But the editor sees many sentences that need commas and some that have commas in the wrong places. You are the editor. Put in commas where they are needed:

I like eating and sleeping‸but John prefers

to starve and read all night.

and take out commas that are not needed:

Lucy/ate a frog.

HINT: Commas show *pauses: I write as well as I can,* (pause) *but editing helps to improve my papers. Yes,* (pause) *my friend stole the elephant.* You almost always pause where two complete sentences are joined by *and, or, but,* and *for.* And you usually pause after *yes, no, however, therefore, for example,* and *well* at the beginnings of sentences. Read the sentences aloud quietly and listen for pauses.

Well I'm a casual sort of person and I want to let you in, on a few secrets of success. First never get too uptight about your work see? For example don't let worry, cause you to lose sleep, because that will make you dull, the next day. However don't sleep all the time friend or you'll never have a chance to study. Instead study hard, but then take some time for relaxing if you get what I mean. To sum it all up, try to achieve the right balance, between work and play for if you don't you'll be a flop understand? <u>You</u> understand but not everybody's that bright!

EXTRA Write a paragraph of your own that needs editing for commas. Give it to a classmate to edit.

COMMAS FOR INTRODUCING AND FOR INTERRUPTING

Words such as *therefore,* and phrases and clauses that introduce a sentence, are usually set off by commas. So are expressions that interrupt the flow of a sentence:

Unfortunately, my dog bit Mike.
Under the apple tree, three mice played and squealed.
Because she is French, her accent is charming.
His name, believe it or not, is Xonx.

HINT: Commas mark pauses. They often come in pairs as in the last example above.

Edit the passages below for commas.

1. Since she can't drive she always walks. This, as you can see is hard for an eighty-year-old. However her son it seems doesn't care.

2. Because he's afraid that no one will love him he eats no fat I understand. Therefore he's lost confidence they say and needs help.

3. Jim looked he explained under the bush and found jewels. Because he's honest he turned them in and amazing to say received a large reward.

4. Although the weather was wet Ruby crazy girl left the house without a coat. Soon it started to snow and sleet. The result as anyone could have told her was a bad cold and an absence of seven days I said <u>seven</u> from school. It was just before exams I fear.

5. Listen you fool to what I am saying or else! I mean it see?

Extra Write some passages of your own that contain a mixture of correct and incorrect uses of commas. Give your paper to a classmate to edit.

COMMAS USED WITH APPOSITIVES AND IN SERIES

An adjective, as you know, modifies a noun or a pronoun. An *appositive* is a phrase that also modifies a noun or a pronoun. Here's a sentence with an appositive:

Cows, very useful animals, have boring personalities.

In the preceding sentence the phrase *very useful animals* is an appositive. Notice that the phrase has a comma before it and a comma after it. All appositives are set off by commas. (If an appositive comes at the end of a sentence, it has a comma before it and a period after it.) Commas also separate items in series:

Cows are useful, boring, slow, and contented.

Edit the passage below by inserting commas where needed.

Dogs cats horses mice and hamsters are animals I like. My mother a woman who always loved animals had a lot of influence on me my brother my seven sisters and about fifteen cousins. She was passionate about animals her best friends. In fact, I sometimes wondered if she liked admired praised loved and even adored them more than her husband children brothers and sisters. However, she had a heart so full of love affection warmth and sympathy that there was room in it for all. Therefore, today a grown person I feel lucky that Mother a true lover of all life filled me with such warmth enthusiasm and sympathy. Now I can adjust to anything, even dogs cats horses and hamsters. That's why people call me Sam the person who loves you him her them it us everything everybody and even myself.

EXTRA Write a passage with appositives and series, but no commas, and give it to a classmate to edit.

CAPITALIZATION

Read the passage below and find the errors in capitalization. Correct the passage, using the two editor's marks shown at the right.   ≡ /

The first sentence of the passage (but not the title) has been edited for you.

HINT 1: All sentences should begin with a capital letter.   ✍ **HINT 2:** Proper names begin with a capital letter *(Robert, Ada Lewis School, India;* but not *my mother, the school, our nation).*   ✍ **HINT 3:** The first, last, and all major words in a title are capitalized *("How the Little Boy Is Growing Up").*

some facts about The world

the Earth is a huge Ball, eight Thousand miles in diameter, Covered with Water, Rock, and Soil.   it is surrounded by the Atmosphere, which is about 125 Miles thick, Made up mainly of Nitrogen and Oxygen, and extremely cold at its Outer Edge.   at the opposite extreme is the Center of the Earth, the inner core. this Core begins 3,200 Miles below the Surface and is 1,600 Miles in diameter.   the Temperature at the Very Center is, perhaps, 9000 degrees fahrenheit.   the Circumference of the Earth is about 25,000 Miles, So that if you drove around the Equator at 500 Miles a day, The Trip would take you about seven Weeks.   however, you couldn't Drive Because about three-Quarters of the Planet's surface at the Equator is Water.

in fact, the Earth is almost entirely covered with Water.   only Thirty Percent is Land.   the deepest part of the oceans is named challenger deep.   it is in the pacific ocean Southwest of the Island of guam and is

CONTINUED

almost Seven Miles deep.   the highest Point on the earth is mount everest, which is Almost five and one-half Miles high.   the earth Rotates on its Axis once every Twenty-Four hours (one Day), and revolves around the sun at eighteen and one-half Miles per Second.   it gets Around once every 365.25 Days, which is called a Year.

how Old is the Earth?   it's probably four and one-half Billion Years Old, About sixty million times as Old as You will be when You die, if You live an Average Life of seventy-five Years.   that makes You feel pretty Young, Doesn't it?   however, You're not too Young to enjoy Reading all about it in a Book called <u>easy Information about The earth and space</u>, by gregory F. shoemaker.

EXTRA Write a passage or several separate sentences containing errors in capitalization like the ones in the passage above. Give it to a classmate to edit.

Lesson 32

QUOTATIONS

Often editors see that writing can be made more interesting if it contains *direct quotations*. Direct quotations tell exactly what someone says:

Tom said, "Bob, please fall through the floor."

Indirect quotations tell what someone said but not in the speaker's exact words:

Tom asked Bob to fall through the floor.

Below are five passages of indirect quotations to be edited into direct quotations. The first two have been done for you. You do the next three.

After the five short passages, there are two longer ones. Edit them so that they contain both direct and indirect quotations. When you finish editing, copy all seven passages over in final draft form.

HINT 1: Enclose the words spoken in quotation marks. **HINT 2:** Quotation marks almost always appear in pairs, before (") and after (") the spoken material. Commas, periods, question marks and exclamation points that punctuate what is spoken go inside (before) quotation marks at the end. **HINT 3:** Use commas to separate all such phrases as *he said, she asked,* and so forth, from the words spoken. **HINT 4:** Start the first word spoken with a capital. **HINT 5:** Start a new paragraph every time there is a new speaker. Now study 1 and 2 below. Notice carefully how the editor used marks to change the passages. Some words were changed, some were deleted, and some were moved. Now edit 3, 4, and 5. Then try 6 and 7.

1. Robert shouted that Gloria should drop dead!

2. A man asked President Lincoln how long a person's legs should be! Lincoln replied that they should be long enough to reach the ground.

3. He asked her please to be more careful in the future.

4. The teacher told the class to break up into small groups for discussion of the book. Then John protested that he hadn't read the book so how could he discuss it.

5. A family was at a restaurant. The waitress asked how they wanted their steaks. The mother said she wanted

CONTINUED

hers medium. The father also asked for medium. However, the son said trustingly he wanted his large.

6. Mrs. Smith was visiting an art class and saw Sally painting a picture. She asked Sally what it was a picture of. Sally replied that it was a picture of God. Mrs. Smith then told Sally that nobody knows what God looks like. Sally looked up and said confidently that they would know when she had finished the picture.

7. Maria asked Ann to go to the beach with her to see some whales. Ann said that if there were whales on the beach they would scare all the people away. Maria explained that the whales weren't on the beach but swimming in the ocean. Ann said she wondered where they got bathing suits big enough.

Extra Write a passage about a conversation. Use only indirect quotations. Give it to a classmate to edit by changing some of the indirect quotations to direct quotations.

Lesson 33

HYPHENS AND COLONS

The hyphen (-) has many uses. So does the colon (:). The passages below need to be edited for the correct use of hyphens and colons. The **Hints** will remind you of some uses of these punctuation marks. When you edit the passages, you'll need to delete some hyphens and colons and add or replace others.

Hint 1: Hyphens are used at the end of a line to indicate that a word has been divided between syllables. Examples: *con-tain, sci-ence, af-ter.* ✍ **Hint 2:** Hyphens connect such prefixes as *all, ex,* and *self* to other words (*all-American*). ✍ **Hint 3:** Many spelled-out numbers are formed with hyphens (*sixty-one*). ✍ **Hint 4:** Colons announce lists (*Bring the following:*). ✍ **Hint 5:** Colons follow salutations in business letters (*Dear Ms. Jones:*). **Hint 6:** Colons separate hour and minute (*6:25 P.M.*). ✍ **Hint 7:** Colons separate chapter and verse (*Genesis 2:7*).

1. Ex champion Cooke, a self made man, now weighs ninetyfour pounds. He likes his new job and is at work at 7-30 each-day.

2. All American athlete Robin Coe read from Proverbs 23,12, the following "Pay attention to your-teachers and learn all you can."

3. The letter read thus "Dear Mom: I'm a self pitying fool. At 5,30 this morning, exactly fortytwo terrible minutes after waking-up, I decided to come-back home. Love: Jim."

4. Never-never forget your: mother, father, and school-friends. If-you-do, you may lead a very-unhappy life, and that's too-bad.

Extra   Write some passages with mistakes in the uses of hyphens and colons land give your paper to a classmate to edit.

PRONOUNS

A pronoun is a word used in place of a noun. Many writers misuse pronouns. They may write *I* instead of *me,* or *them* instead of *they,* or *whom* instead of *who.* Edit the sentences below to correct the pronoun usage. You'll need to change some words and edit others.

he
^*him*   *her's*

HINT 1: Pronouns have a subject form: *He* is going. *Who* is there?   ✍ **HINT 2:** Pronouns have an object form: George scolded *them* (object of verb). Give it to Sue and *me;* I was the one to *whom* she gave it. (objects of prepositions).   ✍ **HINT 3:** The possessive form of a pronoun never uses an apostrophe: *Hers* is prettier than *theirs* or *ours.*

1. Don't ask Jack and I who the dog belonged to. It was her's.

2. Whom do you think did that to John and I? Him and I were standing beside Gloria and she. Suddenly Gloria and her hauled off and hit the teacher, John, I, a dog, and them. So it's Gloria and her, that's whom. Just ask me!

3. You and me should tell Bob and she about brains. Their's are better than ours, her's is best of all. She is so smart it gives he and I a pain just to think about it and her. Him and me work so hard, and us get D's. Him and me think marks should be based on all that effort of our's. Whom else works so hard? To who should A's be given? To we!

EXTRA Write some sentences containing lots of pronouns, some wrongly used. Give them to a classmate to edit.

Lesson 35

THE AGREEMENT OF SUBJECT AND VERB

Singular subjects take the singular form of verbs:

One *boy runs* fast.

Plural subjects take the plural form:

Two *boys run* fast.

Keep the following passage in the present tense. Edit it so that the subjects and verbs agree. The first two sentences have been done for you.

HINT: Subjects such as *one, either,* and *neither* are singular: *One* of the cows *gives* milk. *Neither* of the children *likes* grits.

Four friends ~~is~~ ʌare camping on a high pass near the Continental Divide. To the east, streams and rain flows to the Atlantic Ocean. To the west, they flow into the Pacific. This thought are very exciting because not one of the group have been on the Divide before.

After dinner one night they all does different things. Pat sit by the fire and toast marshmallows. Ann get water from a stream and wash dishes. Irma read a book about wildflowers.

Alice, the strongest, decide to climb a little peak to the north. She have no trouble reaching the top and look down on her friends. They is now crawling into their sleeping bags. She begin to feel the cold sunset wind that blows out of the west. She decide to run back to camp. At first all the paths is easy to

YOU ARE THE EDITOR COPYRIGHT © 1981

CONTINUED

find, but then she realize that one of the turns were wrong.   She is in a strange place.   She have heard about people who panics when they gets lost like this, and she start to shiver.   Both fear and cold causes her to tremble.   But finally she finds the right path and rejoin her friends just before dark.

EXTRA Write a passage in which some subjects and verbs do not agree. Give it to a classmate to edit.

THE TENSE OF VERBS

Edit the following passages so that the tense of the verbs is correct. *Tense* comes from a Latin word meaning "time." Basically there are three tenses: past, present, and future. Unless there is a reason to change, all verbs in a passage should be of the same tense.

Here's an example of mixed tenses. Notice how the sentence reads before and after editing:

At 6:05, John will go to see his dog; at 6:10 he *will* petted him; and at 6:15 he *will* feeds him.

The sentence was edited from future, past, and present tenses to *all future*. Often, however, there *is* a reason for changing tense: *He left yesterday* (past), *but tomorrow he will stay* (future).

1. There were three tenses in language, and they will be past, present, and future. One of the troubles I will always have was keeping to the same tense. Reading this, you could have seen, I still had the trouble. Maybe tomorrow Miss Smith finally teaches me.

2. "I came, I will see, I conquer." That's what the famous Julius Caesar will say when he was defeating his enemy. The three short statements will say a lot.

3. An eight-year-old girl will show her artwork to a visitor, and the visitor compliments her on an excellent drawing of a dog. The girl says, "I really can't draw a dog, so when I will have to draw a dog, I was drawing a horse, and it will come out looking like a dog." "My!" the visitor will say, "how cute!"

4. Yesterday, he will think how good he feels, and he laughs.

EXTRA Write a passage entirely in the present tense and give it to a classmate to edit into entirely past tense, or the other way around.

Lesson 37

THE BUSINESS LETTER

Edit the business letter below for punctuation and capitalization.

HINT 1: In addresses, use commas to separate the town from the state but not the state from the zip code (Dallas, TX 75217). ✍ **HINT 2:** In dates, use a comma to separate the month and day from the year (June 20, 1984). ✍ **HINT 3:** Start the words in the salutation with a capital letter; use a colon (:) after them (Dear Dr. Fox:). ✍ **HINT 4:** Begin the first word in the formal close with a capital letter, but use small letters for the other words. End with a comma (Very truly yours,).

                                        6337 Gravers Avenue

                                        Smithfield NJ, 07703

                                        May 31 1983

Mr. Gerald F Crowd

Youth employment Division, Yankee Clothes Co.

1732, Pine street

Baton rouge LA, 70805

Dear Mr crowd,

      Thank you for your letter. I expect to be in Baton
rouge on june 9. I shall be Very Glad to see you then,
at 9-45, A.M.

                                        sincerely Yours.

                                        Oswald O. newbold

Extra Write a business letter than needs editing for capitalization and punctuation. Give it to a classmate to edit.

Lesson 38

PUNCTUATION AND CAPITALIZATION REVIEW

The following story has correct spelling and paragraphing, but it contains many errors in punctuation and capitalization. Use your knowledge and editor's marks to correct the mistakes. Take your time and work carefully. There are about 125 corrections needed. When you've finished editing the story, copy it in final-draft form on another sheet of paper.

<u>The secret Intelligence of dogs.</u>

most people think. That dog's are less intelligent than Human Beings.   I know otherwise, dogs just act less Bright, in fact dogs minds are much Better than peoples.   Theyre just too bright to act bright.   this conversation in Our House will prove it I think

My Mother looks very worried.   She says to me, "I'm so stupid I didn't Get any bitty-bits for fido."

Fido replies cheerfully.   With a wagging tail, "Woof!   Woof!   I am unhappy.   I say to mom, "but we Just cant let fido starve!

Fido gets up and licks my hand.   And says. "Woof!   Arf!

Well," Groans Mom, "i've got to get your little Sister from her music lesson.   youll just have to climb on your bike.   And ride to the store.   For some bitty-bits."   "but mom I've got a lot of Editing Homework to do."   I moan.

Fido says Arf!   Arf!   and licks.   My hand.

CONTINUED

Go!   says Mom.   "Never mind the editing first

things first

So what do you think happens.   Ill tell you what

happens.   Fido woofs a few more times.   And lies

down with a happy sigh.   To go to sleep.   Meanwhile

however I get on my bike and risking failure in editing

Ride three Miles to the store,

when I get back.   Fido is just waking up from his

nap he wags his tail, arfs cheerfully.   And gets his

Blasted Bitty-Bits.   my Mother comes back with my

Sister Then my Father comes in late and angry.   From

teaching school and marking papers?

Dogs are so dumb" says my Sister.   When she

hears the story.   People are dumber I say, and I go

off miserably.   Passing Fido who is wellfed.   And

looking as if he is asleep on the soft living room

Rug.   When nobody is looking.   He winks at our

cat.   Who smiles back

WORD ORDER IN SENTENCES I

Up pick please eggs those you were enough clumsy to drop John on the floor, please.

Nobody would ever write a sentence like that, but here's the way an editor might straighten it out using circles, arrows, and editor's marks:

Up pick please eggs those you were enough clumsy to drop John on the floor, please

The edited sentence reads: John, please pick up those eggs you were clumsy enough to drop on the floor.

Here's another example. Notice that the editor has added the word *for* but has not changed the meaning of the sentence.

ORIGINAL:

We threw the horse over the fence some hay.

EDITED:

We threw *for* the horse over the fence some hay

The edited sentence reads: We threw some hay over the fence for the horse.

Edit the following sentences so that they say what you think the writer meant them to say. You may add, change, or subtract a word or two, but don't change any ideas. When you have finished editing, copy the sentences in final-draft form on another sheet of paper.

1. All students should study before watching TV two hours a night if they want to do well in school.

2. Please send me instructions how for to make health bread in the enclosed envelope, please.

3. There's a not finer city police chief than Joe O'Malley in the country according to experts.

CONTINUED

4. Your idea will be considered by the principal for solving the lateness problem.

5. Jill scolded the boy who disapproved of his actions.

6. When I tried I got scratched to remove the cat's bowl.

7. Marlene sent the suits to the cleaners that were dirty as a favor to her father.

8. Chris found the boy who had lost his way with the help of the Girl Scouts.

9. Ann fed the child who didn't want her to go hungry.

10. Mr. Toll's influence was great and admired much on his students by all the parents.

EXTRA There are seven places where *only* can be placed in the sentence below. Each placement gives the sentence a different meaning. Draw arrows from *only* to each place and number each arrow. Be prepared to read the seven different versions aloud and to explain the meaning of each.

only

She scolded the little child last week.

WORD ORDER IN SENTENCES II

Editors often change the order of words in sentences to make the meaning clear. Sometimes they edit just to make a sentence sound better. To do this, they use circles, arrows, transpose marks, and other editor's marks.

ORIGINAL:

The river we ate our picnic down by.

EDITED:

The river we ate our picnic down by.

The edited sentence reads: We ate our picnic down by the river.

Edit the sentences below. Use circles, arrows, transpose marks, and, when you need them, other editor's marks.

1. Please under the table go.

2. Very nice to all of us my mother is.

3. I simply why you do it cannot understand.

4. Josh really, my best friend, is quite bright.

5. Look the table under and find some money you will.

6. Circles and arrows use to put in order words.

7. Our teacher harder works than the students do.

8. Never again please do that to me.

9. Then she laughed aloud, and first Molly quietly giggled.

10. To read books in the library is a very good place.

Extra Write some sentences in which the word order sounds wrong or makes the meaning unclear. First, try editing them yourself to be sure it can be done. Then give the unedited sentences to a classmate to edit. Check later to see if you both edited them the same way.

Lesson 41

TRANSITIONS

Each of the four passages below contains two or more ideas. However, the writers have failed to take the reader smoothly from one idea to the next. Moving from one idea to the next is called *transition*. Edit each passage to ensure good transitions. If necessary, you may combine sentences and add words. This passage has been edited to show you how:

Our dog barks, *but* ^She doesn't bite. *Therefore* ^She's

useful but harmless.

HINT: Some transition words you may use are: *although, and, but, even though, furthermore, however, nevertheless, on the other hand, since, so, thus, while.*

1. My mother is strong, forceful, and loud. My father is tender, cooperative, and quiet. I love them both. I hope they don't change.

2. A tough math course may be good for very able students. Molly knows a boy who broke under the strain of such a course.

3. Knowing how to spell is an advantage in life. Good spelling has no connection with high intelligence. Most misspelled words are perfectly easy to understand.

4. In February, our new car began to rust. There was a lot of snow and ice. The roads were heavily salted. When we moved to Alabama the rusting stopped. I prefer the North. I love to ski. I choose rust holes and skiing over good paint and no snow.

EXTRA
Write some passages containing ideas that need connecting. Give them to a classmate to edit for smooth, sensible transitions.

DIRECTIONS

Directions for drawing the diagram below should be clear enough that someone could draw the diagram just as it is without having seen it.

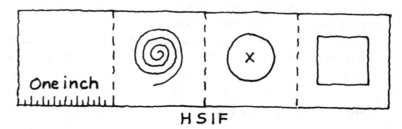

One inch

H S I F

Edit the following directions so that they are clear. Remember to be exact. For example, in the first line of the passage, delete the word *figure* and replace it with the word *rectangle*. You will need to change many words and add many more.

Draw a ~~figure~~ *rectangle* several inches long and one inch

high, lying down.   Divide the figure into four parts.

At the bottom of one part draw an inch.   In the next

part make a curved line going round and round.

Then make a circle, medium-sized, with a little x in

it.   Finally, draw a square in the last part.   Label

the inch.   Below the figure print four letters that

will spell a word backwards.

EXTRA Draw a simple diagram. Write unclear, inexact directions for reproducing it. Give the directions to a classmate to edit. OR: Write inexact, unclear directions for performing an action like tying a shoe, scrambling an egg, or making a telephone call. Give the directions to a classmate to edit.

Lesson 43

DESCRIPTIONS

To describe something well you must use specific words to give important details. For example, "The meal was awful," is not a very good description. A more exact description might say, "The soup was ice cold, the bread was as hard as a hockey puck, and the meat loaf tasted like newspaper."

Below is a picture of a sentence machine and a description of the machine. Edit the description to make it clear, accurate, and complete. You will need to change many words and add many more. Remember your editor's marks. After you've finished editing, copy the description over in final-draft form on a separate sheet of paper.

The sentence machine is old and made of metal. It is fairly large, it stands on legs, and its main part is a sort of bowl. Above the bowl hang two containers. One is full of parts of sentences and the other full of other parts. When a person runs the machine, one container drops stuff into the main part, and the other one drops other stuff. An opening on one side has sentences coming out of it telling what the machine does.

EXTRA Draw or find a picture of a fairly simple object. Write a description of it that isn't very accurate. Give the picture and your paper to a classmate to edit.

THE ORDER OF SENTENCES IN PARAGRAPHS

Editors try to make sure that ideas are written in a sensible order. In each of the five paragraphs below, the sentences are out of order. Edit the order of the sentences by writing the number *1* at the start of what should be the first sentence, the number *2* at the start of the second sentence, and so forth. Use a pencil so that you can erase if you change your mind. When you're done, read aloud (quietly) your reordered version. If need be, edit some more. Then copy the final version on a separate sheet of paper. In passage 1, the first sentence has been numbered for you. In passage 3, the first and last sentences have been numbered.

Hint: Each of these paragraphs should begin with a *topic sentence* that states the general idea of the paragraph.

1. I've eaten dozens and enjoyed every one.   The main dish is always hot and well seasoned.   Finally, the dessert is rich and tasty. ①I don't agree with people who complain about airplane meals. Therefore, give me an airplane meal over home cooking any day!   The salad is always cold, crisp, and full of fresh vegetables.

2. First, older people are respected and helped. They are treated with good humor and kindness. Further, the young are bossed around by everybody. Also, the elderly have beautiful memories to comfort them in troubled times.   Let me explain why I'd much rather be old than young.   On the other hand, the young have to worry about the future.   Hardly anybody respects youthfulness anymore, and youngsters have to do all the work.   That's why I hope to grow old fast and stay old long.

CONTINUED

3. First, good spelling usually makes a good impression on other people, and misspelling makes a bad impression. Second, it is a sad fact that many people think that poor spellers are stupid. If you make a good impression, you are likely to do better in almost every way. Lots of good spellers aren't always bright, and many poor spellers are quite bright. But that doesn't seem to change what so many people think. ⑧So, if you want the best chance to be accepted and to get a job, work on your spelling. And if people think you're stupid, they are less likely to hire you for a job. ①Unfortunately, knowing how to spell correctly is an important advantage in life.

4. The sounds of the radio also keep my own thoughts from turning bad and making me feel very low. The music and talk that come out of it comfort me. These sounds shut me off from all the trouble of the nasty world. Wherever I go, I like to have my portable radio with me, turned on loud. If people knew, they'd get a radio too; then we'd all be happy and nobody would hurt anybody. They just don't know what my beautiful radio is saving me from. Therefore, when people on buses and city streets give me dirty looks, I ignore them.

Extra
Write a simple, carefully ordered paragraph. Begin it with a topic sentence. Then rewrite it so that two or more sentences are out of order. Give it to a classmate to edit.

name:

THE ORDER OF PARAGRAPHS IN A PAPER

Editors read long papers carefully to see that the ideas are arranged in a way that makes good sense. Usually, the main ideas are organized into paragraphs. It's important to have the paragraphs in the best possible order.

Here are five topics for paragraphs on the subject, "The Usefulness of Earthworms." Edit the topics into good order by numbering the five blanks 1 through 5.

The Usefulness of Earthworms

_____ how earthworms help plants grow

_____ what earthworms are

_____ how earthworms help us catch fish

_____ summary of why we should be thankful for earthworms

_____ how earthworms are useful to birds

Many paragraphs begin with a topic sentence that suggests the main idea of the paragraph. Here are five topic sentences for five different paragraphs. Put them into the best order by numbering the five blanks 1 through 5.

Exercise Is Good for You

_____ Of course, you should not overdo exercise.

_____ So you see, most people who exercise live longer and feel better.

_____ Most people don't get enough exercise.

_____ Exercise benefits not only the body but also the mind.

_____ Here are some kinds of exercises that are good for you.

CONTINUED

Here are the topic sentences of the paragraphs in a longer paper. Edit the order of the paragraphs by numbering them 1 through 10.

TV Is Bad for Your Education

_____ Further, the tube can cut you off almost entirely from books and homework.

_____ I'll admit, however, that some programs are educational.

_____ The average American has watched 18,000 hours of TV before graduating from high school.

_____ Obviously, it's important to stop and think and discuss if one is to do well in school.

_____ Thus, watching TV becomes a habit long before the child starts school.

_____ One reason for the trouble is that too many parents want their kids to be quiet and to stay out of the way.

_____ A part of the problem is that parents, too, are TV addicts.

_____ What, then, are the effects on the mind of the TV addict?

_____ But what you can learn from TV doesn't make up for the harm too much watching causes.

_____ To summarize, I'll state seven key words that prove the case.

Extra Make up ten topic sentences for an out-of-order paper and give them to a classmate to put into order. The easiest way is to write them in the right order first, then scramble them.

PARAGRAPHING IN A PASSAGE

At the right is the beginning of an outline for an essay on the topic, "Marks: Good or Bad?" Below is the first part of an essay written on the basis of the outline. The passage should contain four paragraphs, but the writer has used poor judgment. Show where you think new paragraphs should begin:

ꟼ

and where there should be no new paragraphs:

∼ (run in)

To help you, the first two marks have been made.

OUTLINE

I. Introduction: the problem

II. What marks are
   A. Letter systems
   B. Number systems

III. Arguments in favor of marks
   A. Give definite information
   B. Motivate students to study
   C. Needed as records

IV. Arguments against marks
   A. Schoolwork too complicated to be marked
   B. Cause harmful competition
   C. Cause pressure, cheating

<u>Marks: Good or Bad?</u>

Should schools give marks or not?   Some parents, teachers, and even students like marks and demand that schools give them.   Others feel that marks are harmful in many ways. ꟼ Before we go further, let's look at the two main marking systems. One system uses letter grades: A, B, C, D, and F — A meaning "excellent" and F meaning "failure."   Another common system uses numbers, usually from below 60 to 100.   Below 60 means "failure"; 90 and above means "excellent."

CONTINUED

Now, what are the main arguments in favor of marks?

First, they give information about how well a student is doing. Second, marks make students work.

They make students study harder. Third, marks are needed for records so that teachers in the next grade can know what each student needs.

Also, when students change schools, the new school will have records to help put each student in the right class. The arguments against marks are quite strong too. The first is that schoolwork is very complicated.

Therefore, a simple mark isn't enough to describe all the work students do in a subject. Further, marks cause students to compete with each other in harmful ways. Third,

If students are marked, they are likely to feel great pressure from classmates and from home.

This will cause some of them to cheat, and that doesn't help learning at all.

EXTRA Write an outline and then write a well-organized essay based on the outline. Copy it over, with mistakes in paragraphing, and give the copy to a classmate to edit.

Lesson 47

CHOOSING SUBJECTS TO WRITE ABOUT I

Part of an editor's job may be to help writers choose things to write about. The best subjects for you to write about are:

1. Things you know a lot about or have strong ideas or opinions about: and
2. Things you may not know much about but are interested in and can learn about easily (by asking others or by reading books).

Look at the subjects below. Mark each one in box I with a 3 (something you know about), a 2 (something you can easily learn about), or a 1 (not a good subject for you).

After you've marked box I for each subject, pretend you are one of your parents. Mark each subject in box P as your parent would.

Then pretend you are your teacher, and mark each subject in box T as you think your teacher would.

	I	P	T
1. tests, grades, and cheating in school	☐	☐	☐
2. the importance of good manners	☐	☐	☐
3. the world in the 1950s	☐	☐	☐
4. Is the President doing a good job?	☐	☐	☐
5. mistakes parents make in bringing up children	☐	☐	☐
6. the history of England	☐	☐	☐
7. how TV affects schoolwork	☐	☐	☐
8. the importance of having a best friend	☐	☐	☐
9. the trouble with teasing	☐	☐	☐
10. the life of a whale	☐	☐	☐

Extra
Make up some more topics and rate them. Discuss your ratings with your parents, teacher, and other students.

CHOOSING SUBJECTS TO WRITE ABOUT II

It's important for writers to choose subjects that aren't "too big." "Life," "People," and "Science," for example, are huge subjects. An editor would suggest making them smaller and more specific: "Why Teasing Hurts"; "Uncle Max and His Monkey"; "Useful Plants in My Neighborhood."

You are the editor. Look at each of the twelve titles below. If a subject is too big, change it by writing a new title. If a subject doesn't need changing, mark it *OK*.

1. The First Frog I Ever Picked Up

2. Teachers

3. Arms versus Legs

4. Writing Papers for School

5. Two Rules That Need Changing at Our House

6. Work

7. Monday, Tuesday, Wednesday, Thursday, and Friday

8. Seen While Sitting on the Curbstone

9. Noses

10. My Ideas about What Is Important in Life

11. The Day I Failed to Stop a Sneeze

12. Energy Problems and the World's Future

EXTRA Think up five topics that are too broad and write them on a piece of paper. Then, for each broad topic, think of a smaller, more specific one. Give a list of your first five topics to a classmate to find five smaller ones. Compare results.

BEGINNINGS

Some writers have problems beginning their stories or essays. Sometimes they start too fast and don't give enough information. This kind of beginning can confuse the reader, who may have trouble understanding what is happening. More often, writers begin too slowly, writing much more than they need to. This kind of beginning is usually boring to the reader.

Look at the beginnings below. If they need improvement, edit them. You may delete words or even whole sentences; you may add words and sentences. You may replace poor words with better ones. If you think any of the beginnings are good as they stand, mark them *OK*. The first beginning is edited for you to suggest how to go about the task.

HINT 1: Don't say, "I'm going to write about . . ."—just write.   **HINT 2:** Sometimes it works well to begin with a strong statement or question that will arouse the reader's interest.

1. ~~I want to tell you about a very interesting thing~~ that ~~happened to me~~ a few days ago. ~~It has to do with~~ my courageous cat and a very fierce, cowardly dog. ~~They~~ met on the way to the same trash can.

2. Seeing as I am not an authority on this subject, I shall write on another. What I know most about is fish. They fascinate me, totally.

3. What better way to get someone to change her mind than to face her with facts? That's what Bob did after lunch when he met Sue.

4. For breakfast on Saturday morning we had orange juice, blueberry pancakes, syrup, milk, and all the raisins we wanted to fill us up. Saturday was the day of the donkey race, and Friday night my donkey Crumbles had been even more stubborn than usual. So this morning I was worried. Crumbles, though, didn't

CONTINUED

have a worry in the world. I sometimes think I worry too much. She was grazing quietly in the pasture, and her calmness made me angry. She likes breakfast too, even though it's only hay. "Well, Crum," I said, "this is your day—or else!"

5. I got the facts for this paper from the following books: The Remarkable Firefly, The Wonders of Lightning Bugs, and How Fireflies Work. First let me tell you some facts I think you will like. The fire of a firefly is caused by five chemicals in its belly. When these are set off by a sixth chemical, the firefly lights up. And why? Flashing light is the way male fireflies find females. Isn't that interesting?

6. I have no trouble getting along with people. It's ghosts who cause all my problems. If you think this means I'm crazy, you may be right, but let me tell you about it first.

7. Teaching school is not nearly as easy as some pupils seem to think it is. It really is too bad that people can't try harder to be helpful to each other. That would make teaching school easier. It took teacher James Drick three periods of his first day on his first job to find that out. The problem wasn't his personality or bad students, but something else.

EXTRA Write a couple of good beginnings of papers and a couple of poor ones. Without saying which are which, give them to a classmate to edit.

Lesson 50

WORDS AND TONE TO SUIT READERS AND PURPOSE

Editors sometimes notice that writers use words and groups of words that don't sound right for their readers. Edit the passages below by deleting words or phrases that you think don't suit the readers. (Look up the words you don't know in a dictionary.) Some deleted words will have to be replaced. Here's an example.

Mrs. Reed's chalkboard note to seventh graders:

Dear ~~children~~ *students*: Hurry to your seats~~, like nice little~~ ~~people.~~ We have ~~such~~ an exciting ~~little~~ game to play if you all *can keep quiet* ~~are very good little people.~~ ~~Your loving~~ ~~teacher.~~ Thank you. —Mrs. Reed

1. **Principal Gray to students:** Warning! Any brat in this joint found masticating gum will be required to make a visitation to my administrative headquarters. —Charlie G., Your pal

2. **Fire drill notice in fifth-grade homeroom:** Attention Requested!!!! In case of conflagration, duly proceed down the main corridor to the second red-colored door, turn to your left (not right), descend the stairway, and continue walking along quietly to the automobile lot, all the while paying attention to special directions.

3. **Request to parents from eighth-graders:** Dear Mommies and Daddies, We would just love to have your help for our nifty little class play, get it? We implore you to share with us kiddies any articles of clothing that could be employed as costumes for

Lesson 50

CONTINUED

pirates. Oh dear, we forgot to inform you that our dramatization is entitled Watch Out for Pirates! —Your Loved Ones

4. **Space-war action in an adventure book:** The invading aliens didn't move at first. But then they began to go slowly toward the people. When they got nearby they moved very rapidly forward.

Marsha spoke to them, "Stop!" But she could tell they weren't going to discontinue.

Then a man said at the top of his voice, "End the lives of them all! Assassinate these aliens and we'll move rapidly to their ship!"

Marsha revolved to see who had spoken loudly. It was the person whose sister had been made very uncomfortable. Then some of the people began to use their guns. The aliens leaned down under the laser fire. Oh, boy, how exciting it was! Then all became noiseless.

5. **Note from teacher inviting Mr. Jones, the principal, to visit a class:** Oh Principal! My fifth-grade darlings are laying a lot of trouble on me. Please, oh please, when you've nothing better to do, get yourself down here to take in the scene. Yours truly would be extravagantly grateful for your aid and assistance. —Mr. Fred F. Ponderous

EXTRA Write passages that sound wrong for the intended readers. Give them to a classmate to edit. Be sure to tell who the readers are.

Lesson 51

EXACT WORDS

Editors know how to change dull, inexact words and phrases to interesting, exact ones. For example:

A playground: ~~The girl went~~ up the ~~thing~~.
Maxine scrambled clumsily *jungle gym*

Examine the eight sentences below. Delete the underlined words or phrases and replace them with better words or phrases. (You may need to delete or change some words that aren't underlined.)

1. **At a fire:** The <u>man</u> <u>went</u> into the <u>building</u>.

2. **At the zoo:** A <u>person</u> <u>spoke</u> to an <u>animal</u>.

3. **At a swimming pool:** <u>Four girls</u> <u>went</u> under a <u>floating object</u> and <u>came</u> up beside <u>someone</u> who <u>made a noise</u>.

4. **At the airport:** <u>Some things</u> <u>passed by</u> the <u>place</u> while <u>she</u> was <u>standing</u> <u>there</u>.

5. **A thank-you note:** I was <u>glad</u> to have the <u>gift</u>, and you are very <u>kind</u> to give me <u>something</u> so <u>nice</u>.

6. **A description:** The <u>dog</u> was <u>big</u> and <u>made a terrible noise</u>.

7. **A dream:** The red <u>car</u> was <u>moving</u> toward me, and I <u>was</u> on the edge of <u>high</u> place holding onto my <u>toy</u>.

8. **In a kitchen:** He <u>cooked</u> <u>meat</u>, <u>cooked</u> <u>vegetables</u>, and <u>made</u> <u>dessert</u>.

EXTRA Write a passage with lots of dull words in it and give it to a classmate to edit.

Lesson 52

THE TONE OF A BUSINESS LETTER

Tone is the way writing "sounds" to a reader. Writing often needs editing so that it will sound right. Below is a business letter that needs to be edited for tone. Edit it so that it sounds serious and businesslike. On a separate sheet of paper copy the edited letter.

HINT: A business letter should be clear, factual, and brief. Even if the writer is feeling angry, the tone should not be emotional.

Dear Ms. Silken:

I'm very angry, and when I get angry I stay angry. Your company mailed me four Best Cotton T-shirts, at $4.75 each, but you scums charged me for a dozen, that is cool a $57!! Please (and if you don't I'm going to sue you; my father is a lawyer) accept my check for $19 in full payment. If there is any difficulty about this, watch out! My spies sometimes get to your part of the country.

Affectionately (ha! ha!),

Vicia Strongtemp

Extra
Write a business letter that needs editing for tone. Give it to a classmate to edit.

Lesson 53

COMBINING SENTENCES I

Writing usually sounds best if it contains a variety of sentences—some long and some short. When writing contains too many short, choppy sentences, editors combine them into longer ones. Here are two examples. Read each aloud twice, once as it was before editing, once as edited.

Teaching ∧is a hard job∧ It is not for lazy people.

The parrot squawked∧ *and then* It flew ~~away// It went~~ into

its cage.

Now, edit each of the items below into one sentence. Use the examples above to help you decide how to combine sentences.

1. Mrs. Smith spoiled Jim. Jim was her favorite son.

2. I try to avoid John. The reason is that he has such a bad temper.

3. The house collapsed. It was when the thieves were hiding in it.

4. I don't like peas. However, I eat them to earn my dessert.

5. Skiing can be very risky. Slopes are steep. Snow is slippery.

6. Here is why I admire Jenny. She never does less than her best.

7. The Herbert Nelson School is an excellent school. It's where my grandfather was a pupil. Also, my Aunt Meg taught third grade there.

8. The monkey's mother was killed. The monkey soon died too.

EXTRA Write several items with two or three short, choppy sentences. Edit each item into one sentence. Then give an unedited version to a classmate to edit. Compare the two editings.

YOU ARE THE EDITOR COPYRIGHT © 1981

COMBINING SENTENCES II

The passage below is written with too many short, choppy sentences. Edit it by combining some of the sentences so that it reads more interestingly. You'll need to change some punctuation. For example:

School begins today ^*and* Kevin is happy.

His vacation was boring. There was

nothing to do but read ^*and* ~~He also~~ watched

TV. He missed all his friends ^, ~~He~~ missed

sports ^*and* ~~He~~ even missed homework.

~~He was~~ *That* surprised ^*him*.

HINT: Read the passage aloud (quietly) to "hear" what needs changing. Change some words, delete some, add some, but don't change the ideas.

I come home after school. I am always hungry. I rush for the refrigerator. Sometimes I don't even see Mom. She has been waiting. She wants to welcome me. My stomach blinds my eyes. I hurt her feelings. I shouldn't do this. Really I'm glad to know Mom cares. One day I passed her. As usual I went to the fridge. I happened to look around. Mom was laughing. She was also crying. I was amazed. I went back to Mom's chair. I kissed her on the top of the head. I smiled. I said, "Hi, Mom!" You should have seen her expression. It was on her face.

Extra Write a passage in short, jerky sentences. Edit it for sentence variety. Give an unedited copy of the passage to a classmate to edit. Compare the two editings; they will probably be somewhat different.

Lesson 55

SENTENCE VARIETY

Some writers have the problem of stringing too many words and ideas together into a single sentence. Most good writing has a variety of sentences—some long and some short. Editors can help writers create sentence variety. You are the editor. Edit the passage below, which is written as one long, strung-together sentence. You'll need to add and delete words and to change punctuation and capitalization.

First, here's an example of how to do this. Notice carefully how the passage was written before it was edited and what changes the editor made:

> Mrs. Jones was an understanding but strict teacher, and she sometimes wrote messages on the chalkboard, and one The I remember best was written after recess, because the class had been thoughtless, so and the message said, "It's safe to make mistakes in this class, but it's best if you make a different mistake each time," and I've remembered it all my life.

HINT: Editors often read writing aloud to "hear" how it sounds; usually it sounds best with long sentences and short sentences mixed together.

> I remember when I first tried to ride a bicycle, because it was a very painful experience, and I was only four years old at the time, so I wasn't very well coordinated, and I had no idea how to balance myself, with the result that I no sooner had climbed on the bike than I was back on the pavement, and I started crying and kept crying louder and louder, and yet I wanted to try it again, when I saw my father

CONTINUED

walking up the street, coming home from work, and he was always very helpful to me, but he was firm, too, because he felt I should not be spoiled but should learn as much as possible on my own, so he smiled and asked, "Having trouble?" and I sniffled tearfully, "Yeah, I feel awful!" so he told me to get up, pick up my bike, and listen to him, which I did, and then he slowly pushed me along, holding the bike up and showing me how to steer and lean to balance myself, and the first thing I knew he was ten feet behind me, and I was steering and balancing on my own, so I gave a great shout of triumph and immediately crashed again, but it wasn't long before I was riding by myself all over the neighborhood, and I felt very thankful that my father was such a good teacher, and so was my mom thankful because she liked to have a little peace, which she got now that I was on wheels and falling down only now and then.

EXTRA Write a passage in one long, strung-together sentence. Edit it for sentence variety, just to be sure it can be done. Then give an unedited copy of the passage to a classmate to edit. Compare the two editings; they will probably be somewhat different.

RHYTHM AND FLOW USING PARALLEL CONSTRUCTION

Reading some sentences is like riding on a bumpy road. Here is an example:

"I came and then, when I had seen, I was able to conquer."

That sentence bumps along and doesn't flow well. The word *flow* means to move smoothly from word to word or phrase to phrase or idea to idea. The Roman Emperor Julius Caesar said the same thing:

"I came, I saw, I conquered."

Here's how Caesar might have arrived at his sentence:

I came, ~~and then, when~~ I ~~had seen~~, I ~~was~~
                    saw
~~able to~~ conquer.
              ed

Caesar's sentence uses *parallel construction,* meaning that each verb in the sentence is in the same form (in this case, the simple past tense): *came, saw, conquered* (not *came, had seen, was able to conquer*).

Parallel construction doesn't apply only to verbs. Look at the following sentences. See how the editor has changed them using parallel phrases *(of the people, by the people, for the people):*

Abraham Lincoln favored government of the

people, ~~thought it should be~~ by the people, and

~~He wanted it to benefit~~ the people.
                            for

Edit the following passages using parallel construction so that they flow well. Then on a separate sheet write each in final-draft form.

1. Gravelle is the woman with the long blond hair, and who had a chirpy voice. Her face is also very strong.

2. When Bob saw Verne, she was smiling, looked lively, but also Bob thought she seemed very sad and appeared to need rest.

Lesson 56

CONTINUED

3. Playing soccer is fun, to play the piano is more fun, and hooky is the most fun of all to be played.

4. Because he had never felt a snake, and a reason was that he also felt scared of animals, and in addition timidity was a part of his character, so he ran away screaming.

5. The children enjoyed it when they messed up the house, breaking toys, playing loudly when the baby was sleeping, they came home late for supper, and, worst of all, lies were told by them.

EXTRA Write a passage with good flow and rhythm. Then rewrite it without parallel construction and give that version to a classmate to edit. Compare results.

Lesson 57

CUT WORDINESS

Some writers use too many words. Editors delete needless words to make the writing crisper and more interesting:

One ~~single~~ brave, ~~courageous~~ warrior killed

the great ~~big~~ creature~~, dead.~~

Edit the wordiness out of the following passages. (In some cases you may want to delete several needless words and replace them with one new word.)

1. It's a fact, and there's no doubt about it, and no one disagrees on the matter, that Lance is conceited and stuck-up.

2. This is a car which caused a lot of trouble and difficulty the whole entire time Mr. Jones owned and drove it anywhere.

3. That is a matter I absolutely refuse to discuss to talk about.

4. Klondike School, which is the finest school for all purposes in the whole region, selects all of its teachers with care. It is a fine school also because it pays them well, which is a good thing.

5. It is nice that he can take a joke on himself at his own expense, and that is one real reason that I admire him.

6. The farmer planted seeds in the ground under the dirt, then watered them every day with water until they sprouted up out of the earth.

Extra Write several passages that have extra, needless words and give them to a classmate to edit.

Lesson 58

FORMAL AND INFORMAL WRITING

The characters above are reacting *informally* and *formally* to a ball breaking the window. Writing, too, can be formal or informal. In formal writing you choose your words to sound serious and respectful, and you don't use slang. Informal writing may use slang and other words and phrases to sound friendly and relaxed. You'd write a formal letter to the Queen of England. You'd write an informal note to your best friend.

The first five sentences below are informal writing. Edit them into formal writing. The next three are formal. Edit them into informal writing. Sentences 1 and 6 have been done for you.

INFORMAL REACTION

FORMAL REACTION

Informal to Formal

1. ~~Let's scram~~ *We must leave* before we ~~get pinched~~ *are arrested* by the ~~cops~~ *police.*

2. My mom bugged me no end about my no-good pals.

3. That cat is really into books instead of the tube.

4. George hits the sack early so he can get plenty of shut-eye.

5. Mayella just can't stand people who keep yakking all day long instead of picking up a few bucks.

Formal to Informal
(Look up unfamiliar words in the dictionary.)

6. ~~Robert~~ *Bob* will ~~request~~ *ask* Ann to ~~make her departure immediately~~ *leave right now.*

7. At the Smith residence, dinner is served precisely at 6:30.

8. Relating to others requires a maximum effort to understand their circumstances.

EXTRA Write two formal sentences, and edit them into informal English. Then write two informal sentences and edit them into formal English. Now give your unedited sentences to a classmate to edit. Compare results.

Lesson 59

DEVELOP INTEREST AND CUT DULLNESS

Editors remind writers to cut out what is boring or useless in their writing. Editors also remind writers to develop the more interesting parts. To *develop* means to "add more facts and details."

In the following passage several things need to be cut out. Other things need to be developed. Edit the passage by underlining once what should be developed. Then write *dev* in the margin. Underline twice what should be cut and write *cut* in the margin. Also show where new paragraphs should begin. One *cut* and one *dev* have been done to show to how.

cut

dev

That morning I got up at 8:00, about thirty minutes later than usual, because I usually get up at 7:30. I had a delicious breakfast. Then I hurried down the steps, fell, and hurt myself. Later, all confused, I saw a guy leaning against a doorway. He spoke to me and pulled a knife. I gave him my money. Then I went on toward school thinking what I would tell my friends whose names are Susan, Doris, Abbie, Mike, Leo, and one whose name I can't spell. I was so worried that I almost got run over by a bus, and the driver swore at me. I didn't bleed much when I banged into the lamppost. I now had four streets to cross to get to school, Arch Street, Vine Street, Race Street, and Main Street. When I finally got to school, everybody looked at me, asked me questions, and even insulted me.

EXTRA Write a similar passage for a classmate to edit. OR: Rewrite part or all of the passage above, cutting and developing as you think best. Make up the specific details you need.

Lesson 60

PROOFREAD
FOR CARELESS ERRORS

The last step in editing is *proofreading*. Proofreading involves looking over a paper and correcting any mistakes that are left, no matter how small.

Proofread the passage below. The content does not need changing. However, there are more than sixty mistakes you'll need to fix with editor's marks. When you've finished, copy the passage on a separate sheet of paper and proofread your copy.

Heping an Ol Man in Touble

One Saturdy morning som Cub Scout were Late to theire den meetinge.   Th den moher asked, "Wy are you So late?

Oh," sad a bight small boye, "wee wer hellping and old man cros the steet"

"Thats verry kinde" Said the deen mothere "but thate shoudent make you half an houre lat.   Whey are you so lat"

Th boy's lookd at eache other withe muche emmbarrassment.   The brigh boy pokd an largeer boy whoo lookt brave.   Hee smiled att the floar and, thenn at th den moher.   Well," he said "the olde mann diddn't want want to go"

Extra   Write a paper very clearly. Then add a number of careless errors. Have a classmate proofread and correct it.

Lesson 61

EDIT FOR STYLE: A REVIEW

The passage below is an editorial to be published in a school newspaper. It will be read by students, teachers, and parents. It needs editing badly. You are the editor, and your job is to edit for *style* so that the writing will be suitable for its readers. For example, you would edit out phrases such as "Gee whiz!" or "That's neat-o!" However, do not cut out or add any ideas. Mark two or three places that should be developed (write *dev* in the margin). There are about a dozen wordy places to shorten, two or three sentences to cut out, and several words that need replacing. Also, paragraphing is needed. There are no spelling or punctuation errors in the passage.

The first three sentences have been done for you. Also the first *dev* is marked. Since different editors will edit differently, use your own best judgment. (Look up unfamiliar words in the dictionary.)

Honesty or ~~Crooks and Liars~~ *Dishonesty* in the Seventh Grade?

It's hard to tell the truth, hard to resist cheating, and hard not to steal, but dishonesty has ~~proceeded excessively~~ *gone too far* in our seventh grade. ~~Man, I really mean it.~~ Hardly *a week* ~~seven days~~ or even *a day* ~~twenty-four hours~~ passes without ~~that~~ some *student doing* ~~skunk does~~ a dishonest act. Let me prove it. Over half the *students* ~~kids~~ in the class said that *their possessions* ~~stuff of theirs~~ had been *stolen* ~~snitched~~ during the month of February 1980. Remember the example of the evil theft that happened? And absolutely nobody ever tells the veracity when it comes to what concerns work done at home. People are better at false excuses than true work. What can we do about the nefarious situation that faces us all? First, we must follow the guidelines. I mean the guidelines of the student-teacher committee. This is

dev

CONTINUED

the committee that met.   It met last week.   Second,

each individual, single person should promise three

newly established kinds of behavior: to tell the truth,

never to steal, and not to be dishonest.   It is my

genuine opinion that honesty can become a habit—

if we work on it and if we encourage each other.

The good habit can drive out the bad.   We must do

it!   Otherwise, our class has a sad future.   I mean

a sad future as a class and as individuals.   Wow!

Come on, kids, let's go!

EXTRA Make up details and develop the spots you marked *dev*.
Then copy the editorial as a final draft and proofread it. OR: Write a
passage that needs editing for style and give it to a classmate to edit.

name: _____

TEST I: DO YOU KNOW YOUR EDITOR'S MARKS?

Directions: In the left column there are sixteen statements. Each tells what a certain editor's mark does. In the two right columns there are three editor's marks for each numbered statement. Decide which is the correct mark for each statement and circle A, B, or C. Try this sample:

0. Use a capital letter.   0. A ⟨mark⟩ B ⟨mark⟩ C ⟨mark⟩

The correct answer is B. Circle the B.

1. Put a period here. 1. A ⟨mark⟩ B ⊙ C •

2. Add something here. 2. A ∧ B ⟨mark⟩ C stet⟍

3. Start a new paragraph here. 3. A ⟨mark⟩ B ⟨mark⟩ C ⟨mark⟩

4. Transpose letters or words. 4. A ✗ B ⟨mark⟩ C ⟨mark⟩

5. Delete or remove something. 5. A ✗ B ⟨mark⟩ C ⟨mark⟩

6. Put an apostrophe here. 6. A ⟨mark⟩ B , C ap

7. Change a letter. 7. A ⟨mark⟩ B # C ⟨mark⟩

8. Use a capital letter. 8. A ⟨mark⟩ B ⟨mark⟩ C ⟨mark⟩

9. Put a quotation mark here. 9. A " B ⟨mark⟩ C qu

10. Close the gap. 10. A # B ⟨mark⟩ C ⟨mark⟩

11. Keep the deleted material. 11. A stet⟍ B ∧∧∧ C _____

12. Run lines together; no paragraph. 12. A ⟨mark⟩ B ⟨mark⟩ C ⟨mark⟩

13. Remove the item and close the gap. 13. A ⟨mark⟩ B ✗⟨mark⟩ C ⟨mark⟩

14. Make a space here. 14. A ⟨mark⟩ B / C #

15. Use a comma here. 15. A ⟨mark⟩ B ⟨mark⟩ C ,

16. Use a small letter. 16. A ⟨mark⟩ B # C ⟨mark⟩

TEST II: HOW WELL CAN YOU EDIT A PASSAGE?

A class was given the assignment of writing an essay about a personal experience. The best papers would be published in the school magazine. Here is one of the papers that was written. It is printed on the following page. As you will see, it needs some editing.

This is your editing test. Edit the paper for spelling, punctuation, capitalization, paragraphing, and word choice. Look at the underlined parts numbered 1 through 36. Decide what editing is needed for each. Then, following the test, on pages 88–89, are the answer sheets. For each item on the test there are three editing choices that have the same number as the underlined part on the test. Circle the correct one, A, B, or C after each number.

Here's a sample item, number 0. Choose either A, B, or C:

Jim knew (0) hed never bee (0) the same.

0. A hĕd never bee
    B hĕd never beȩ
    Ⓒ hĕd never beȩ

The contraction *he'd* needs an apostrophe and *be* should have only one *e*. So C is the correct answer. Circle the C.

At (1) The Auto repair (1) Shop

When (2) me and Mom (2) take our new car into the shop for a checkup, there's (3) alway's some crummy (3) suspense. Will it need anything serious? If it does, will it cost a lot of money? We always know there are a few little (4) troubles a stuck (4) latch, (5) a rattle a cieling (5) lamp that's out, and that strange noise deep inside when you stop or start quickly.

I'll begin with the first act. We get up (6) early on saterday (6) morning to be the first in line at the service desk. But when we finally arrive (7) there's always some people (7) ahead of us. "They must spend the whole night (8) hear, I ex- (8) plain to Mom.

"You're not kidding, Sallie," she groans, and we stand and (9) wait. At lest we (9) get to the desk, and a man in a greasy shirt asks us to list our troubles, which we do. "It all sounds pretty routine," says the man, "except for that noise deep inside. That could be bad."

"Is the body falling off?" (10) I investigate him. "No, (10) he says, "but it could be a lot of things."

We look sadly at each other, and Mom explains that we'll wait, and she asks how long he thinks it will be.

"Maybe a couple of hours," (11) the dope protests, looks (11) over Mom's shoulder. "Next!" (12) he shouts. the 2nd action (12) is the two-hour wait. We both brought books to read, so we (13) sat down, and try (13) to concentrate. The trouble is there's so much noise and talk about clutches, gears, (14) tires, stupid grinding noises, (14) wheels out of line, lack of pep, (15) and so forth. That (15) I wonder why people don't all go back to walking. (16) Also I cant con centrate (16) on my book. I get (17) pretty inpatient, and tell (17) Mom I'm going to wander around a bit. She's deep in a story and (18) doesnt seem to here. Now (18) we come to the third act. I've wandered outside and then into the repair shop. I see a whole line of cars, most of (19) them with its hoodopen. (19) They remind me of enormous, hungry zoo animals waiting for the keeper to throw some food into their mouths. Some of them (20) is eating the heds (20) of mechanics, I imagine, but the mechanics always come out, heads on. And what a lot of (21) noises there are. (21) My ears are being killed by clanks, whirs, squeals, and grinds. Every now and then a machine gun goes off or an enormous (22) snake invisible to I hisses. (22) Suddenly my eye catches sight of our car, and I start (23) perambulating over to them (23) to ask the man how he is getting along.

"Hey, kid," somebody yells, grabbing my arm, "get out of here! (24) You want get to hurt." (24)

"Oh, no, I'm sorry," I say to a small frowning man in overalls, and I walk back to the waiting (25) room. All most getting (25) knocked over by cars squealing into repair (26) slots. Act four are (26) the climax. We have been reading for (27) anouther hour. When a (27) voice yells, "Mrs. Bradley?"

Mom looks up, catches the man's eye, and goes over to the desk. (28) "How did we do, she states." (28)

"Well, my friends, not badly," (29) he smiled. "every things (29) covered by the guarantee, except for the oil change and lube. The cashier has your bill."

Mom sighs with relief and (30) started over to the cashiers (30) window, but suddenly I think of something. "What about the deep noise inside? Isn't (31) thatsome trouble." (31)

The man smiles, reaches behind the (32) counter. And lifted (32) up an object with wheels. "Do you recognize this?" he asks.

I feel myself turning red with (33) embarrassment. Oh gee," (33) I say, "it's my careless little brother's red wagon."

(34) "Well, remove it away, (34) the man says, laughing. "Small wheeled items in the car trunk can make very mysterious sounds when you start and stop. And, by the way," (35) he added, "we dont (35) charge for removal of red (36) wagons." THE END! (36)

name: _____

TEST II ANSWER SHEET

Circle one letter for each item.

1. A The Auto repair
   B The Auto repair
   C The Auto repair

2. A (me and Mom)
   B me and Mom
   C me and Mom

3. A always some crummy
   B always some crummy
   C always some crummy

4. A troubles a stuck
   B troubles a stuck
   C troubles a stuck

5. A a rattle a cieling
   B a rattle a cieling
   C a rattle a cieling

6. A early on saturday
   B early on saturday
   C early on saterday

7. A there's always some people
   B there's always some people
   C there's always some people

8. A hear I ex-
   B hear, I ex-
   C hear, I ex-

9. A wait. At lest we
   B wait. At last we
   C wait. At last we

10. A I investigate him. "No,
    B I investigate him. "No,
    C I investigate him. "No,

11. A the dope protests, looks
    B the dope protests looks
    C the dope protests looks

12. A he shouts. the 2nd action
    B he shouts. the 2nd action
    C he shouts the 2nd action

13. A sat down and try
    B sat down and try
    C sat down, and try

14. A tires, stupid grinding noises,
    B tires, stupid grinding noises,
    C tires, stupid grinding noises,

15. A and so forth That
    B and so forth That
    C and so forth. That

16. A Also I cant con centrate
    B Also I cant con centrate
    C Also I cant con centrate

name: _____

17. A   pretty inpatient, and tell
    B   pretty inpatient, and tell
    C   pretty inpatient, and tell

18. A   doesnt seem to here. Now
    B   doesnt seem to here. Now
    C   doesnt seem to here. Now

19. A   them with its hoodopen.
    B   them with its hoodopen.
    C   them with its hoodopen.

20. A   is eating the heds
    B   is eating the heds
    C   is eating the heds

21. A   noises there are!
    B   noises there are!
    C   noises there are.

22. A   snake invisible to I hisses.
    B   snake invisible to I hisses.
    C   snake invisible to I hisses.

23. A   perambulating over to them
    B   perambulating over to them
    C   perambulating over to them

24. A   You want get to hurt."
    B   You want get to hurt."
    C   You want get to hurt."

25. A   room All most getting
    B   room All most getting
    C   room. All most getting

26. A   slots. Act four are
    B   slots. Act four are
    C   slots. Act four are

27. A   another hour. When a
    B   anouther hour. When a
    C   anouther hour. When a

28. A   "How did we do she states."
    B   "How did we do she states."
    C   "How did we do, she states."

29. A   he smiled. "every things
    B   he smiled. "every things
    C   he smiled, "every things

30. A   started over to the cashiers
    B   started over to the cashiers
    C   started over to the cashiers

31. A   stet   thatsome trouble."
    B   thatsome trouble."
    C   stet   thatsome trouble."

32. A   counter. And lifted
    B   counter. And lifted
    C   counter And lifted

33. A   embarrassment. Oh gee,"
    B   embarrassment Oh gee,"
    C   embarrassment Oh gee,"

34. A   "Well remove it away,
    B   "Well, remove it away
    C   "Well remove it away

35. A   he added, "we dont
    B   he added "we dont
    C   he added "we dont

36. A   wagons." THE END
    B   wagons." THE END
    C   wagons." THE END

EDITOR'S CERTIFICATE

THIS IS TO CERTIFY THAT

_____

HAS BEEN AWARDED THIS CERTIFICATE OF EDITORIAL COMPETENCE

FOR HAVING DEMONSTRATED THE ABILITY TO RECOGNIZE WHAT

EACH EDITOR'S MARK DOES, AND TO EDIT WITH REASONABLE

COMPETENCE A LONG PASSAGE, AND THUS IS PREPARED

1. TO IMPROVE HIS OR HER OWN WRITING, AND

2. TO HELP OTHERS IMPROVE THEIR WRITING.

_____
NAME OF AWARDING OFFICIAL

_____
NAME OF SCHOOL

_____
DATE

WRITER/EDITOR'S HANDBOOK

This handbook is for you to use when writing and editing. You should keep it at your desk while you're writing at school. And you should take it home with you when you have writing or editing homework.

Go through it once or twice to become familiar with its contents so you know what's in it. Then use it as a reference book—like a dictionary or an encyclopedia—to look up things you need to know about good writing and editing.

Contents

A SELF-EDITOR'S CHECKLIST: BEFORE BEGINNING THE PAPER

Before you start to write, you will save yourself time and trouble—and do a better job—if you ask yourself these questions:

1. **Assignment:** Do I understand exactly what the assignment is? Do I know its purpose and what I'm supposed to do?

2. **Length:** Do I know about how long the project is supposed to be? Is there a maximum or a minimum length?

3. **Importance:** Is this a very important paper, worth a lot of my time and effort? Or is it a not-so-important paper that I can do rather quickly?

4. **Audience:** Do I understand for whom I'm writing this paper? How can I satisfy my readers?

5. **Ideas and information:** Do I have enough ideas and information to write the paper? Can I easily find more information? Are there people I can talk to who will give me information for the paper? If not, should I seek another subject?

6. **Organization:** Have I thought about the best way to put my ideas together? Have I jotted down a few notes about my ideas to guide me?

7. **Getting started:** If I'm having a hard time getting started, can I simply start writing freely, in any part of the paper? Do I remember that I can always rewrite, revise, and reorganize?

8. **Due date:** Am I sure about when the paper is due and how much time I have to complete it? Have I planned so that I can get it done? Have I left enough time for editing and revising?

EDITOR'S MARKS

mark	meaning	example of use
ℐ	Delete the material; remove.	ℐtelephone call ~~call~~
◡	Close the gap.	grand‿mother
ℐ	Delete the material and close the gap.	her's; grandson
stet ----	Put back the deleted material.	*stet* Don't you ~~ever~~ do that again!
∧	Add a letter, a word, or other material.	Bush∧teeth.
∧	Change a letter or letters.	She's a bad gal.
#	Make a space.	the evening∧meal
∩	Transpose letters or words; reverse the order.	editor
∧	Add a comma.	cats∧mice, and dogs
⊙	Add a period.	Mr⊙Fox slept⊙
∨	Add an apostrophe.	Don∨t hit me, please.
≡	Make the letter a capital.	his mother. then he ...
/	Make the letter small.	My /Brother's fists /Hit me.
¶	Start a new paragraph.	"Go," said Mary. ¶"Yes," I said.
⸢⸣ ⸢⸣	Add a quotation mark.	"Go, said Mary.
⌐	Run in the two lines; no new paragraph.	His mother loved all animals. That's why she loved John.

PUNCTUATION AND CAPITALIZATION RULES

PUNCTUATION

Periods

Use periods:

1. at the ends of sentences, except question and exclamation sentences:

    I am the editor.

2. after abbreviations:

    N.Y. (New York)   Dr. (doctor)   gals. (gallons)

3. after numbers and letters that label items:

    I. A. 1. a.

Commas

Use commas:

1. to separate two sentences joined by *and, but,* or *for:*

    Ozzie sang merrily all morning, but Isabel just groaned.

    NOTE: (1) Use no comma if the sentences are very short:
    Ozzie sang and Isabel groaned.

    and (2) Use no comma in a sentence with a single subject and a compound verb.
    Ozzie sang merrily all morning but merely groaned in the afternoon.

2. to set off phrases called *appositives:*

    Editing, *an extremely useful skill,* should be taught in all schools.

3. to set off introductory phrases or clauses:

    Between our house and yours, a high fence would help.
    Because we fight so much, boxing gloves would help.

4. to set off names in direct address:

    George, show me your paper.
    Come here, *Mugsie,* and be quiet.

5. to set off certain words when they are used alone at the beginning of a sentence (listen for a pause):

    No, I won't go.   *However,* I'll send Frank.   *Well,* he's very brave.

6. to set off interrupting expressions:

    His papers, *I'm glad to say,* are fun to read.
    Hers, *on the other hand,* are very dull.

7. to set off clauses that aren't necessary to the meaning of a sentence:

    Our car, *which we bought yesterday,* clanks and bangs on hills.
    Our dog, *who runs away whenever she can,* had six puppies.

    Without the clause set off by commas, the sentences still make sense:
    Our car clanks and bangs on hills.
    Our dog had six puppies.

    NOTE: If a clause is necessary to the meaning don't use commas:
    Cars *that clank and bang* need repairs.

    Without the clause the meaning of the sentence is completely different:
    Cars need repairs.

8. to separate items in a series:

> The editor inserted *commas, periods, long words, too many capitals, and a lot of nonsense.*

9. to set off each item after the first one in dates and addresses:

> He was born on *Sunday, July 4, 1873,* at noon.
> Editors slave away at *6 Davis Drive, Belmont,*
> *California 94002,* and also at home till late at night.

> NOTE: Put no comma between state and ZIP code number.

10. in dialogue, to set off the words spoken from those that tell who spoke them:

> George said, "I love you."
> "Grunt, grunt," remarked the pig.

> NOTE: Use no comma if a question or exclamation is spoken:

> "Did you ring?" asked the butler.
> "Get out!" screamed Ollie.

11. after the salutation of a friendly letter and the close in all letters:

> Dear Molly,   Sincerely yours,

Quotation marks

Use quotation marks:

1. to indicate spoken words:

> Mike said, "We slept well."
> "Do I understand," asked Jill, "that I owe ten cents?"

2. to quote words in your writing:

> The point is well made by Frank Harris: "Strong men are made by opposition."
> She's always saying "far out" in her conversation.

3. to make the titles of chapters, stories, or articles in books or magazines:

> In *You Are the Editor,* there is a section called "Writer/Editor's Handbook."
> NOTE: End quotation marks usually follow other punctuation.

Exclamation marks

Use exclamation marks:

1. at the ends of exclamations—words intended to show strong emotion or emphasis:

> Oh, no! The mice are eating the orchids!

Colons

Use colons:

1. to announce that something follows:

> Her feelings were many: rage, pity, revulsion, and fear.
> Please bring these items: a pencil, some paper, the new handbook, and your brain.

2. after the salutation in a business letter:

> Dear Sir: Dear Ms. Bligh:

3. in writing the time or to indicate chapter and verse:

> 7:30 P.M.   Genesis 4:12

Hyphens

Use hyphens:

1. to divide a word at the end of a line, between syllables:

    Please don't always keep talk-
    ing while I'm interrupting.

2. to write out compound numbers:

    twenty-six

3. after prefixes such as *all, ex,* and *self:*

    all-American   ex-husband   self-employed

CAPITALIZATION

Always capitalize:

1. the pronoun *I:*

    After I learn to edit, I will edit you.

2. a name or a proper noun:

    Chris   Africa   France   Missouri

3. the names of months, days, and holidays:

    April   Tuesday   Yom Kippur   Easter

    NOTE: Don't capitalize the four seasons:

    spring   summer   fall   winter

4. names of organizations or brands:

    the American Red Cross   Glasser Middle School
    the Bell Telephone Company   Ford cars   Gooey Chewies

5. the names of races and nationalities, places, religions, special events and periods of history, and documents:

    Caucasian, Canadian, Brazilian; Central Park, Pacific Ocean; Catholic,
       Baptist; World War I, the Middle Ages; the Constitution, the Dec-
       laration of Independence

6. words used as a part of a person's name and showing relationship or position:

    Uncle Jim   Major Fennel   Senator Porter   Superintendent Bask

    EXCEPTIONS: my mother   the principal

7. the first, last, and all important words in a title:

    You Are the Editor
    "What Sue Saw under the Tree"

8. in letters, the salutation and the first word of the close:

    Dear Sir: Dear Minnie,
    Very truly yours,   Yours sincerely,

9. the names of courses (but not the names of subjects):

    Advanced Math I   History of Civilization

    EXCEPTIONS: math   history

10. in dialogue, the first word spoken:

    "Look at me," he said.
    "Please remember," she said, "that he is a teacher."

    NOTE: In general, capitalize all names.

SIX USEFUL SPELLING RULES

1. *ie or ei*

    When sound is ee, put *i* before *e* (*fierce, believe*) except after *c* (*receive, ceiling*). When sound is not ee, put *e* before *i* (*height, weight*). Here are two sentences of exceptions: He *seized* (n)*either weird leisure* (*ei* words pronounced ee), but his *friend sieved* the *mischief* (*ie* words not pronounced ee).

2. Words ending with silent *e*

    Words that end with silent *e* (*taste, hope, nerve*) drop the final *e* before a suffix beginning with a vowel (*ing, ed, ous*), as in *tasting, hoped, nervous*. *Exceptions:* words that end with *ce* or *ge* when adding *able* or *ous*: *noticeable, courageous*. (The *e* keeps the *c* and *g* soft.) Also, the words *ninth* and *truly*.

3. Doubling the final consonant

    When one-syllable words (*hit, stop*), and words accented on the last syllable (*remit, occur*), end with a single consonant after a single vowel, double the final consonant when you add a suffix beginning with a vowel (*er, ed, ing*): *hitter, stopped, occurring*.

    NOTE: Exceptions are (1) words with two vowels before the consonant: *seat, seated;* (2) words ending in two consonants: *result, resulting;* (3) words not accented on the last syllable: *opened, benefited*.

4. *y* to *i* and add *es, ed, er, est*

    When you add *es, ed, er,* or *est* to words that end with *y* with a consonant before it, change the *y* to *i*: *cry, cries; reply, replied; silly, sillier; merry, merriest*.

    NOTE: (1) When there is a vowel before the *y* (*toy, valley*) merely add an *s* (*toys, valleys*) and (2) When you add *ing* to a word ending with *y* (*try, study*), just add it with no change (*trying, studying*).

5. Prefixes

    When you add a prefix to a root word, just add it without changing the spelling of the prefix or the root: *mis + spell = misspell; un + needed = unneeded; dis + appear = disappear; re + invest = reinvest*.

6. Suffixes beginning with a consonant

    When you add a suffix beginning with a consonant to a root word, just add the suffix. Don't change the spelling of the suffix or the root: *govern + ment = government; lone + ly = lonely; usual + ly = usually; mean + ness = meanness*.

TOPICS FOR WRITING: SOME STARTERS

Are you ever stuck for a topic to write about? Even professional writers get stuck. Here are some key words and phrases that may help you out. You can use them again and again; each time they may help you think of a good, new topic.

REMINDER 1: A good topic will probably be one you know something about. **REMINDER 2:** Most topics people choose are much too large. The best are usually fairly small and specific.

how to do something
how to make something
a danger, an accident
something good and
    comfortable
what happened on the way
    to . . .
worries, troubles
a face, a hand, an expression
a birthday
a meal, a dish
tests—in school, in life
a joy, a sorrow
what I hear, see, feel now
a character in a book or on
    TV, compared to someone
    else
the effects of a TV program
a victory, a defeat
a game, a contest
music I like, hate
a conflict, an insult
a surprise
an embarrassment
a job I enjoyed, hated
an animal, fish, bird
a good, awful party
a journey
a contest involving people,
    things
a big conviction of mine
escapes
superstitions
a game I, others play
rules, breaking rules
hunting, finding something
a strength, weakness of mine
signals, symbols
stealing
power, weakness
what people hide from
what I believe about . . .

an unforgettable classroom
what makes an enemy
something or somebody that
    changed me
going away, being away
a bad dream, a good dream
a quarrel, an argument
a pest, an annoyance
catching something, catching
    somebody
pleasing others, displeasing
    others
violence, hardship
the best, worst part of the day
a disease, a handicap
climbing something, going down
what annoys me about . . .
on the telephone
twenty-five years from now
a thing, person, place I value
if I found $500 . . .
clothes I hate, love
the worst thing about meals
punishments, rewards
old age, babyhood
being lost, getting found
an ideal or terrible holiday
parents compared to children
babies—human and other
habits—good, bad, amazing
my ambition is to be . . .
an action on the street, at
    home
a neighborhood character
a most disliked place
what needs to be invented
something that could be
    improved
what needs to be destroyed
something that puzzles me
a letter telling a personal
    problem, and the reply

A SELF-EDITOR'S CHECKLIST: BEFORE HANDING IN THE PAPER

Let's assume you're near the end of writing an important paper. Don't make a final copy of it yet. You want to be sure you've done the best possible job of it. It will help to ask yourself these questions before writing the final draft.

1. **Purpose:** Does the paper fit the assignment and my purpose?

2. **Organization:** Are the ideas put together in good order? Does each paragraph have a main idea? Are the main ideas presented in separate paragraphs?

3. **Audience:** Is my choice of words appropriate for my readers?

4. **Selection and development:** Are there parts that need cutting or shortening? Are there parts that need to be developed?

5. **First sentences:** Does the paper start well and catch the reader's interest?

6. **Last sentence(s):** Does the paper end strongly? Does it answer all questions? Will the reader understand my conclusion?

7. **Sentence(s):** Do the sentences flow well? Are there some short ones and some long ones? Are there any fragments or run-ons?

8. **Title:** Does the title catch the reader's interest? Is it appropriate for the paper?

9. **Punctuation:** Is all the punctuation correct?

10. **Capitalization:** Have I followed the rules? Are there any unneeded capitals?

11. **Spelling:** Have I checked every word and looked up words I'm not sure of?

Having answered the preceding questions, make a final copy of your paper, then ask the last question:

12. **Readability and appearance:** Is the paper in the correct form? Is it easy to read? Is it pleasing to look at? Have I done a final, close proofreading?

YOU ARE THE EDITOR COPYRIGHT © 1981

SYMBOLS TEACHERS USE
IN CORRECTING PAPERS

After you edit your paper and hand it in, your teacher "comments" on it. Teachers seldom make changes or corrections. Instead, they usually write symbols in the margin to show what more you need to do, and they underline the troublespots to help you revise your paper. Below are some symbols teachers often use. Many are different from the editor's marks you've learned. When you get papers back from your teacher and need to know what the marks mean, check here first.

SYMBOL	WHAT IT MEANS, WHAT TO DO ABOUT IT
cap	Begin the word with a capital letter.
frag	Sentence fragment. Make it a whole sentence.
gr	Mistake in grammar. Correct it.
H	Handwriting unclear. Make it clear.
K	Awkwardly expressed. Try to say it better.
lc	Lowercase. Use a small letter, not a capital letter.
m?	Meaning unclear or wrong. Make it clear or correct it.
note	Note the change the teacher made.
¶	New paragraph needed here. Fix it. (Be sure you know why.)
no ¶	No paragraph needed here. Fix it. (Be sure you know why.)
p	Punctuation error. Correct it.
ref	What does the word refer to? (For example: Bob and Jim arrived. He looked great.) Correct it: Bob looked great.
rep	Repetition. Doesn't sound right. Find another word or
r-o	Run-on sentences. Two sentences run together; punctuate them as separate sentences.
s-v	Subject and verb don't agree. (For example: The frogs is croaking.) Correct it: The frogs are croaking.
sp	Spelling mistake. Correct it.
T	Mistake in verb tense. Correct it.
WW	Wrong word. Choose a better one.
w.o.	Write it out. Don't use a figure or an abbreviation.
ℓ	Delete. Cut out the letters or words marked.
#	Space needed here. Correct it.
‿	Gap should be closed. Close it.
?	Is this what you mean? Are your facts correct? Correct and make clear.
X	Obvious error. Correct it.
∧	Something left out. Put it in.
dev	Develop. Add more details.
cut	Material is too long or too dull. Shorten or remove it.

YOU ARE THE EDITOR COPYRIGHT © 1981

ANSWER KEY AND TEACHER'S NOTES

Following are answers and teacher's notes for most of the lessons included in *You Are the Editor*. The lessons for which there are no correct or incorrect answers do not appear. Suggested answers are given for those lessons in which correct answers may vary.

PURPOSE: To teach students how to delete, how to close gaps, and how to delete and close

This is the first of eleven lessons teaching fourteen editor's marks. The lessons should be done in fairly quick succession so that students soon may enjoy and practice editing papers with full knowledge of editorial mechanics.

The lesson explains itself, but you may want to read the instructions aloud together in class before students edit the passage. Point out the words spelled correctly (in bold-faced type) so that students will refer to them. (It may be helpful to read the passage aloud so that students get the meaning of it before they start editing.)

Students should correct their own papers as you dictate the answers, reinforcing difficult spots by writing on the chalkboard; or you may duplicate a corrected sheet and give one to each student for self-correction.

Lesson 4   name: 4

DELETE AND CLOSE THE GAP

When you write you sometimes put in letters that should not be there. Editors remove such mistakes by using the *delete* mark (shown at the right). It means "take out" or "delete":

The boy spats on on the floor floor.

Another mark editors use is the *close* mark (shown at the right). It means "close," and it closes a gap that shouldn't be there:

My bed room is some times so crowwded that I must sleep on the car pet.

When a letter is deleted from inside a word, it leaves a gap to be closed:

crowwded sleep delete close

Using delete and close marks, edit the following passage.

Suppose I some how got to to be an editor. I would edit my little brother and and sister out of my bed room. There wouldn't be any gaps to close. In stead, I'd use two delete marks, and that would be all! Of course, Momm and Dadd might not not like it, but I could just just say, "Keep them in side your yours rooms." I'd even sved pay them five dollars a a day for the service, un til I ended up in the the poor house. May be I'd like it there.

Some correct spellings: **bedroom, close, dollars, instead, might, poorhouse, somehow, until, wouldn't**

Extra Write a paragraph that needs lots of delete and close marks. Give it to a classmate to edit. Write very clearly.

page 8   YOU ARE THE EDITOR © COPYRIGHT

Lesson 5   name:

KEEP IT IN   *stet* _____

Sometimes writers or editors take something out (delete), then decide they want to keep it in after all. Here's how they mark what is to be kept:

stet /   My mother was ~~rather~~ angry at me.

The stet in the margin is the Latin word for "stay." The broken line under the letters shows what is supposed to stay in.

Edit the following paragraph for stets. Use one stet in the margin next to each line for each word or group of words you think should stay. For some lines you'll need more than one stet. And in some cases, you may choose not to stet what is deleted.

I'm not ~~certain~~ sure why we have so many ~~lots of~~

stet insects around our house. But I've got ~~a few~~ ideas. It

stet could be because my sister's room is ~~even~~ dirtier than

my brother's. Even my parents are not ~~not~~ a miracle

of ~~complete~~ cleanliness. They've been known to leave

our sink ~~very~~ full of dirty dishes for many days ~~and~~

stet ~~days.~~ Anyway, insects' appetites are ~~surprisingly~~

strong, and they'll march to wherever ~~all~~ food and dirt

are ~~lying~~ lying around. You might call it "the bugs'

stet / stet hunger journey ~~or trip.~~" After ~~all,~~ bugs have to ~~eat~~

too. And there is plenty ~~enough~~ for them to eat

around our house.

Extra Write some sentences or a paragraph that need "keep it in" marks. Give your paper to a classmate to edit.

page 9   *YOU ARE THE EDITOR COPYRIGHT © 1981*

PURPOSE: **To teach students how to reinstate deleted material**

The "stet" idea will probably be brand new to most students, so be sure it is understood. It may be helpful to do the first two lines of the passage aloud to be sure everything is clear.

Explain that, although the stet mark is less frequently needed than the other editor's marks, it is important in preparing final drafts.

Lesson 6   name:

ADD SOMETHING

Writers sometimes leave out necessary letters or words. Editors add what's needed by using a caret mark shown at the right: ∧

som∧thing; ba∧na; Because of mistakes I failed ∧test.

The following passage contains nearly thirty words with a letter or letters omitted and about twenty-five places where a word is missing. Edit the passage using carets to show where to put the needed additions.

Som∧ pe∧ple say that girls ∧ diferent from boy∧. They∧

that girl∧ are gentl∧ and nice, but every boy∧ tough and

rude. Wel∧ maybe that∧ what pe∧ple ∧ saying, but

everybody I know doesn't fit with∧people say. My

friend's sist∧r, ∧ example, whose name∧ Sally, is

extreme∧ strong∧ fierce. She∧able∧beat up boy∧ who are∧

whole year old∧r than she is, and she∧not at all gentle∧

nice. Howev∧r, ∧ does get very∧marks in s∧ool, and

the∧all like her as∧ pupil. On∧other hand, ∧ own

∧other, a boy∧ year older than I, is alway∧read∧ books

and∧gentl∧ and nice except∧ he's mad. Then he laugh∧

very∧and stamp∧ out of∧room. Anywa∧ my id∧a is that

you can't make ge∧ral sta∧ments∧girls and boy∧. You

have∧ask: "W∧ich girl? W∧ich boy?"

Some correct spellings: **different, everybody, general, gentle, idea, people, school, statements, which**

Extra Make up ten sentences with letters and words missing. Let a classmate, using carets to make additions, edit your sentences.

page 10   *YOU ARE THE EDITOR COPYRIGHT © 1981*

PURPOSE: **To teach students how to add letters and words by using carets**

Point out that the caret provides an easy, quick way to correct an omission (a very common error). Be sure students understand the examples. (It may be helpful to read the passage aloud, with omitted words orally inserted, so that students will get the meaning of it before they start editing.)

Students should correct their own papers as you dictate the answers, reinforcing difficult spots by writing on the chalkboard; or you may duplicate a corrected sheet and give one to each student for self-correction. Be sure that students use the bold-faced reference words if they need to.

PURPOSE: To teach students how to indicate that a letter in a word is being changed

Be sure students understand the two uses of the caret (from the Latin word *caret*, which means "is lacking"). Emphasize the importance of their referring to the twenty-four correctly spelled words (in bold-faced type), so that they get practice in seeing and writing the correct spelling, while at the same time increasing their alertness to errors and how to correct them. You may want to duplicate a corrected sheet to give to each student for self-correction.

CHANGE OR ADD LETTERS

You know that editors use carets to add missing letters. They also use carets to correct wrong letters in words:

girl kat studying

Sometimes words have both missing letters and wrong letters. Practice using this editing tool on some spelling demons. First be sure you know the correct spelling of the words. Study the list at the bottom of the page. Now edit the misspelled words below. After editing each word, write it correctly in the blank following it.

already	*already*	excelant	*excellent*
amoung	*among*	expiriance	*experience*
anser	*answer*	familar	*familiar*
argument	*argument*	Ambarrassed	*embarrassed*
busness	*business*	inneresting	*interesting*
captin	*captain*	libary	*library*
colar	*color*	opinon	*opinion*
campletly	*completely*	probaly	*probably*
decide	*decide*	relize	*realize*
develop	*develop*	separate	*separate*
diferant	*different*	suprise	*surprise*
doctar	*doctor*	usally	*usually*

Some correct spellings: **already, among, answer, argument, business, captain, color, completely, decide, develop, different, doctor, embarrassed, excellent, experience, familiar, interesting, library, opinion, probably, realize, separate, surprise, usually**

Extra Write some sentences or a paragraph using all of the above twenty-four words in a way that makes sense. Underline each of the twenty-four words. Try to spell them correctly but, just in case, give them to a classmate to edit.

PURPOSE: To teach students how to edit spaces into sentences

It may help if you have students do the first line, and then go over it with the entire class before students edit the rest of the passage. It is probably not necessary to collect these lessons, as the idea is simple. Reinforce it on the chalkboard in the next few days as occasion arises. Point out that a problem in real writing is knowing when to write a word solid and when as two words (*outside* is one word; *all right* is two). Always write the correct form on the chalkboard and leave it there. (The fable, by the way, is modernized, modified Aesop!)

ADD SPACE

Youmayknowthatsomepeoplemakecareless mistakesandrunwordstogether.

To correct this, editors use the *space* mark (shown at the right). It means "space needed here."   #

Youmayknow ...

Now correct the sentence above, using twelve space marks.

Below is a fable written by a strange person who forgot to leave spaces. To edit it you'll need nearly 140 space marks. Be sure to show a space after each comma and period.

Onherheadacountrygirlwascarryingapailofmilkto markettosell.Asshewalkedalong,shesangamerrysongand busilythoughtaboutwhatwonderfulthingsshewoulddo withthemoneyshewouldget.Shewouldbuyagoodhen,and thelovelyhenwouldlaybeautifuleggs.Theeggswouldhatch intohealthylittlechicksthatwouldgrowupintonicefatbirds thatthegirlwouldsell.Shewouldusethemoneytostartsaving togotoaveterinaryschool.Thenshewouldbeabletocurethe diseasesofallthefarmanimalsandwouldbeveryusefultothe farmers.Thethoughtmadeherlaughoutloudwithpleasure. Shelaughedsohardthatherheadshookandherbodyrocked, andshespilledeverydropofmilk.Themoralis:Don'tcount yourchickensbeforetheyarehatched.

EXTRA Write a brief story. Run all the words together as in the fable above. Give it to a classmate to edit with space marks. Write or print each letter *very* clearly.

Lesson 9

SWITCH THEM

Obviously, this sentence is in very bad trouble. Do you see why?

An editor uses the *transpose* mark (shown at the right) to reverse the order of letters or words. *Transpose* means "switch positions," and the mark works like this:

Obviously, this sentence ...

Now correct the sentence above. You'll need eight transpose marks.

Editors also use transpose marks to change the order of words:

my cat big

Use four transpose marks to correct this sentence:

Now tell me, what did the rug say to the floor? I've got you covered!

Be the editor and correct the following passages. You will need more than forty transpose marks.

After you edit, write (on a separate sheet) the correct spelling of all the words that had reversed letters.

1. Sign in a classroom: It is safe to make a mistake in this classroom, but it is much better for you to make a different one each time. Then you are learning.

2. A third-grader was asked why she did not want to go back to school. She replied, "I can't read, I can't write, and they won't let me talk."

3. Definition of homework: A thing kids don't have any of when it's time for their favorite TV program, but they have great piles of when it's time to go to bed.

4. Riddle: What do elephants have that no other animals have? Answer: baby elephants

Extra Write some short paragraphs containing reversed letters and words. Write very clearly. Give them to a classmate to edit.

PURPOSE: To teach students how to transpose letters and words

Have a student write the sample sentence correctly on the chalkboard as other students use transpose marks to edit it at their seats. (It may be helpful to read all the passages aloud so that students get the meaning of them before they start editing.) To reinforce the correct spelling, be sure students correctly copy the words with transposed letters.

Lesson 10

PAUSE AND STOP

Editors show that a comma is needed by using the *comma* mark (shown at the right). They show that a period is needed by using the *period* mark (shown just below the comma mark). Here is a sentence with commas and a period added:

Please, John, pass the bread.

These special marks make the corrections very easy to see.

In the following passages, all the commas and periods have been omitted. You will need nineteen comma marks and seventeen period marks to correct them.

Hint 1: Most of the time, commas are used to mark pauses.   **Hint 2:** Periods mark the ends of sentences and abbreviations.

1. Our teacher, Mr. J. R. Firmly, came into the room. He looked straight at Molly and said, "Molly, your hands are filthy. What would you say if I came to class with dirty hands like that?"

   "Well," said Molly, "I think, Mr. Firmly, I'd be too polite to mention it."

2. Mrs. Mary R. Jones is a Scout den mother. One day her Cub Scouts were late for their meeting.

   "Boys, you are late," she said. "Please, Jimmy, explain why."

   "Well," said Jimmy, "we were helping an old man cross the street."

   "Very nice," said Mrs. Jones, "but that doesn't take half an hour, does it?"

   "Well," said Jimmy, "we had trouble. He didn't want to go."

Extra Write some passages with commas and periods missing and give them to a classmate to edit. Tell your classmate how many commas and periods you think there should be.

PURPOSE: To teach students how to edit commas and periods into sentences

The lesson assumes your students know something about commas and periods. The *Hints* are only a quick review. If your students need more work on the uses of commas and periods, use the "Writer/Editor's Handbook" (pages 94–95) or use your classroom grammar text. Point out that a comma with a circle around it means a period and that editors recognize it as such. This lesson may be corrected in small groups, with hands raised if your help is needed, or by duplicating a corrected sheet and giving one to each student for self-correction. Remember, the main idea is to learn editing; review of commas and periods is secondary.

PURPOSE: To teach students how to add omitted apostrophes

Be sure that students remember that two uses of the apostrophe are being edited here—possessives and contractions. Refer to your classroom grammar text if more teaching of apostrophes is needed.

ADD APOSTROPHES

When an apostrophe is left out, editors add it this way:

you've

Edit the paragraph below for missing apostrophes.

HINT 1: Apostrophes show what belongs to what or to whom (*the cat's meow, the girls' gym, Mr. Jones's hat, the men's umbrellas*). **HINT 2:** Apostrophes in contractions show where letters have been left out (*she's—she is; can't—cannot; you'll—you will; they're—they are*).

Ill tell you this, today Im very happy. I dont know why, exactly. But I think its because of my teacher. You see, shes teaching me how to edit. Youre probably wondering why that makes me happy. Heres the reason: I love to write, but my writings very sloppy, like my brothers room. Ive got great ideas, but theyre usually lost among all my mistakes.

My teachers always saying, "A persons writing must be clear." Shes right. It doesnt help to have great ideas if people cant understand them.

My teacher also says, "Editings a writers helper." Shes right about that too. And in the same way my brothers room needs a janitor, my writing needs an editor. Since Im learning to edit, Ill be the editor!

Extra Write a paragraph using lots of words that need apostrophes, but leave the apostrophes out. Give the paragraph to a classmate to edit.

PURPOSE: To teach students how to edit capital letters into small letters and vice versa

The lesson explains itself. Use the "Writer/Editor's Handbook" (page 96) if more teaching or review is needed than is given in the *Hints* (or use your classroom grammar text). The lesson may be corrected in small groups, by dictation to the class, or by using duplicated copies of the corrected lesson.

CAPITAL AND SMALL LETTERS

This is how editors show that a small letter should be capitalized:

nebraska

This is how they show that a capital letter should be written small:

Candy

Here's an edited sentence:

my sister amy hates Winter,
But she Loves Jim.

Now edit the passages below for mistakes in capitalization.

HINT 1: Capitalize the first word of a sentence, proper names (*Dallas, Ken*) and proper adjectives (*French, American*), and the names of days, months, and organizations (*Monday, May, the American Red Cross*). **HINT 2:** Don't capitalize seasons (*spring, fall*), or words such as *uncle* or *mother* unless they are part of a name (*Uncle Ben*).

1. the tv Announcer said: "you've heard both our Editorial And a Reply to our Editorial. now Here is Jane Castle, speaking for Those who have No Opinion."

2. he went to california to get into the Movies and He did get In. He Sells Popcorn at a Drive-In.

3. a long-Winded preacher came to Church with a Bandaged Finger. He explained, "you see, I was Thinking about my Sermon and cut my Finger."

after the sermon, a Member said to Him, "perhaps it Would have been Better, reverend jackson, to Think about your Finger and cut Your Sermon."

4. "i hate Wars," Said the Child. "they make too much History."

EXTRA Make up some passages that contain mistakes in capitalization and give them to a classmate to edit.

PARAGRAPHS AND QUOTATION MARKS

Usually, a new paragraph starts when writing shifts from one main idea to another. Editors show that a new paragraph is needed by inserting the *paragraph mark* (shown at the right).

In dialogue (conversation), a new paragraph starts each time a new speaker is quoted:

"You <u>love</u> spinach, Lolly," said Mom. "Yes," said Lolly, "but not enough to eat it."

Also in dialogue, the words people say are enclosed in quotation marks:

"Come on," yelled Sal, "let's get out of here!"

Editors supply omitted quotation marks by using the *quotation marks* (shown at the right).

My mother isn't here, Jones said.

Below is a little story that hasn't been divided into paragraphs. Remember to use the paragraph mark when the main idea shifts or when a new speaker is quoted. If speech is quoted within a paragraph about the speaker, do not start a new paragraph. Also, all the quotation marks have been left out. Edit the story.

Billy was a very spoiled little boy. He refused to eat his food. I won't! I won't! he yelled. You have to or you'll get sick, said his mother. No, yelled Billy, I won't! and he threw the dish across the room. Then his father said to his mother, Let me deal with him. All right, sighed the mother, you can have him. Billy, said his father, you have to eat something or you'll starve. So what do you want? I promise I'll get it for you. Billy smiled wickedly. I want an earthworm, he said. The father gulped but replied, OK, a promise is a promise, and he dug up a worm and put it on Billy's plate. I don't want it!

CONTINUED

yelled Billy. That's not the way I like worms! I like them fried. OK, sighed the father, and he fried the worm in butter and presented it to Billy. It's fried and looks nice, said Billy, but maybe it's poison. Dad, you eat half of it first. All right, Billy, the father snarled, and he cut the worm in half, closed his eyes, and swallowed one half. Oh, no! wailed Billy. I won't eat it. Dad, look what you've done! What's the matter <u>now</u>? moaned the father. Billy shouted, You ate <u>my</u> half!

Extra Write a piece of conversation, either one you've heard or one you make up. Omit all paragraphs and quotations marks. Be sure, though, that the words make it clear who's speaking. Then give your paper to a classmate to edit.

PURPOSE: **To teach students how to edit a passage for paragraphs and for quotation marks**

It will help students with little background in writing dialogue if you emphasize that there are two editing functions: (1) to put in a new paragraph each time the speaker changes, and (2) to enclose all words actually spoken in quotation marks. A few examples on the chalkboard may help. Remember to use the "Writer/Editor's Handbook" (page 95) if more instruction on using quotation marks in dialogue is needed. Some students may be helped if you (or a good student reader) read the passage aloud to show the idea, with the first few editings explained orally as they are written on the chalkboard.

PURPOSE: To teach students how to edit for proper paragraphing

This lesson explains itself. Point out that some students may be used to the mark *no ¶* instead of the mark for run in. Point out, too, that this lesson provides a chance to review other editor's marks and that students should be alert to a variety of errors needing editing.

The *Extra* provides an entertaining homework assignment.

NO NEW PARAGRAPH—RUN IN

Sometimes writers start new paragraphs where they shouldn't. Editors use a *run-in* mark (shown at the right) to indicate that no new paragraph should begin. For example:

Please learn to edit. Editing your writing
gives you courage.
It helps you to write freely and then later to
improve and correct.

Edit the following passage. It needs three run-in marks. There are also nearly twenty other places where editor's marks you've already learned are needed. Add them too.

A problem in our school is littering.
People seem to be too weak to carry papers and
trash to the nearest wastebasket. Instead, theyre
always dropping on the floor of the halls and
classrooms classrooms, and the place rapidly becomes a
mess. Its really disgusting.
One day, two of my friends and I decide to try and
experiment to people teach to stop littering we took a
sheet wrinkled of paper and taped a dollar bill on to it.
We wrote a message right beside the bill
saying, "Congratulations! Youve just done a good
deed by picking up this piece of litter.
This dollar is Reward. also, you are hereby
awarded membership in the Anti-Litter club."

CONTINUED

When no one was looking we placed the piece
paper, dollar down, on the floor. Then we leaned
against wall the and waited.

Extra Finish the story in the same style and then get a classmate to edit the ending you've written.

Lesson 15

name:

REVIEW OF EDITOR'S MARKS I

In the blank beside each editor's mark, write what the mark does. Then give an example. The first one has been done to show you how.

1. ⟋ 1. *delete or remove material*
Example: *dogs*

2. ◯ 2. *close the gap*
Example: *every body*

3. ⟑ 3. *delete the material and close the gap*
Example: *birdd*

4. ∧ 4. *add or change a word, letter, or other material*
Example: *I eat hamburgers*

5. # 5. *make a space*
Example: *allright*

6. ∿ 6. *transpose letters or words*
Example: *one, three, two, four, flan*

7. ⋏ 7. *add a comma*
Example: *birds, cats, and tulips*

8. ⊙ 8. *add a period*
Example: *Mr. Jones went to bed.*

9. ≡ 9. *make the letter a capital*
Example: *andy went to london.*

10. ⫽ 10. *make the letter small*
Example: *I like boats.*

11. ¶ 11. *start a new paragraph*
Example: *"Come," said Fred. ¶ "I can't," said Ike.*

page 21   YOU ARE THE EDITOR COPYRIGHT © 1981

Lesson 15

name:

CONTINUED

12. ⌄ ⌄ 12. *add quotation marks*
Example: *Sally shouted, "Go away!"*

13. ⌄ 13. *add an apostrophe*
Example: *I'll go now.*

14. stet ___ 14. *put back the deleted material*
Example: *I love ice cream very much.* /stet

15. ⌐ 15. *run in the two lines (no new paragraph)*
Example: *Mary went to the store.*
Then she went to the movies.

Words you may need to spell: **apostrophe, capitalize, delete, omit, paragraph, quotation, transpose**

page 22   YOU ARE THE EDITOR COPYRIGHT © 1981

PURPOSE: **To review the use of editor's marks and to ascertain whether students have learned what the marks do** (*Wording and examples may vary.*)

Instruct students to write their explanations and examples very clearly. This is a good lesson to collect and score, giving perhaps 1 point for the explanation and 1 point for the example for a perfect score of 30 points. If you use a marking system in your school, the lesson can be used as a test and given a grade (multiply the score by 3.33 for a grade based on a scale of 100). On pages 85 and 86, there are two editing tests for which this lesson can be a preliminary.)

PURPOSE: To review the use of editor's marks *(Examples may vary.)*

Urge students to write their examples very clearly. If Lesson 15 was used as a test, Lesson 16 may serve as a follow-up, giving students a chance to study to improve their performances. This lesson, too, is suitable for grading. If you give 1 point for the correct mark and 2 points for a correct example, a perfect score is 54. (Multiply the score by 1.85 for a grade based on a scale of 100.)

At this point your students should be ready for Test I: Do You Know Your Editor's Marks? (page 85).

Lesson 16 · name:

REVIEW OF EDITOR'S MARKS II

Here are sixteen statements. Each tells what a certain editor's mark means. After each one, draw the mark and then give an example of how it works. The first one is done to show you how.

1. Make a space. # *My dog has fleas.*
2. Close the gap. ⌒ *bed room*
3. Add a word or letter. ∧ *He ran away*
4. Run in the two lines (no new paragraph). ⊃ *We sang. We danced.*
5. Make the letter a capital. ≡ *look at molly.*
6. Change a letter. ∧ *teacher*
7. Put back the deleted material. stet *stet far away*
8. Start a new paragraph. ¶ *"Go away," Ellen said. ¶ "I won't," Rick said.*
9. Add a comma. ∧ *pigs, dogs, cats, and mice*
10. Delete the material. *frogs sing sing loudly*
11. Make the letter small (lower case). / *Summer*
12. Add quotation marks. ∨∨ *I love you, he said.*
13. Delete the material and close the gap. *dogs*
14. Transpose words or letters. ∼ *if you likes*
15. Add a period. ⊙ *Dr Jones*
16. Add an apostrophe. ∨ *cant*

PURPOSE: To review the rule for adding suffixes to words ending with silent e and to give practice in correcting words to which the rule applies

Before using this lesson, read the general statement about spelling on page 4. Many students will find it useful to go over in class the four *Hints* and to do the first two lines of the passage together before they begin the lesson. Urge students to keep referring to the *Hints* if they are not sure of the spellings. They shouldn't just guess. After students have completed the lesson, check their lists of copied words, discuss the words that several people misspelled. Have students correct words they missed, and then copy the correct spellings.

Lesson 17 · name:

SUFFIXES ON SILENT-e WORDS

The paragraph below contains many silent-e words that end with suffixes. Use delete marks and close marks to edit them:

com ing   care ful

After you've edited them, list the words, spelling them correctly.

HINT 1: Words that end with silent e drop the e before adding a suffix that begins with a vowel (come + ing = coming; nerve + ous = nervous). **HINT 2:** Words that end in silent e keep the e when adding a suffix that begins with a consonant (move + ment = movement; nice + ly = nicely). **HINT 3:** Words such as *noticeable* and *courageous* keep the e to show that the c and g stay soft. **HINT 4:** Exceptions are *truly* and *ninth* (but *ninety*, not *ninty*).

What made the lonely boy truly happy was writing stories. Most of the stories were exciting. He liked creating tales about disasters—about things crashing and coming apart.

One story was about a man driving carelessly down the road at ninety miles an hour. All of a sudden his car started smoking fiercely. The man driving the car immediately slowed down.

At sixty miles an hour the car's engine started flaming. At fifty, the tires exploded, yet the driver didn't seem nervous. At thirty miles an hour the fenders and doors flew off. At twenty, the windows popped out. At ten, the steering wheel began coming off. Finally the car stopped. The driver was unhurt. He sat there smiling.

Some correct spellings: **carelessly, creating, driver, driving, exciting, exploded, fiercely, flaming, immediately, lonely, nervous, ninety, smiling, truly, writing**

EXTRA Write a paragraph of your own containing silent-e words and suffixes. Give it to a classmate to edit.

WHEN TO DOUBLE FINAL CONSONANTS

Some suffixes begin with vowels, for example, *ing, ed, er.* Certain words double the final consonant when adding such suffixes *(skip, skipped).* In the passage below there are many words with suffixes added. Some are spelled correctly and some are not. Edit the ones that are misspelled. After you've edited them, list the words, spelling them correctly.

HINT 1:   Double the final consonant if the word ends with a single consonant and has only one syllable *(hit, hitting),* or if the word is pronounced with the accent on the last syllable *(begin, beginning).*   **HINT 2:**   Don't double the final consonant if two vowels or another consonant come right before it *(fool, fooled; start, started),* or if the word is pronounced with the accent on any syllable but the last *(open, opening).*

Lots of people are jogging today.   I've never liked exercise myself.   I've always preferred eating to sweating.

My friend Alice was an exercise freak.   She started every day with 100 laps in the swimming pool. She ended every day by running two miles.   In between she jumpped rope and lifted weights.

In the beginning, Alice benefited from all her exercise.   When she began she was fatter than I was. Then every day she seemmed to be getting thinner and thinner.   That was fine until she started offerring me advice.

"Look what's happenning to you!" she'd say. "You're so fat your buttons are popping!   How about coming to the gym with me and losing some weight?"

Every time I saw her she patted my stomach.   I felt like hitting her.   And I wasn't the only one.

☞

PURPOSE: To review the rule for doubling final consonants and to give practice in correcting words to which the rule applies

Before using this lesson, read the general statement about spelling on page 4. This is a very useful rule. Go over the *Hints* in class and write on the chalkboard some examples of each category of words. If necessary, do the first few lines of the passage together. Emphasize the importance of referring to the correctly spelled words in bold-faced type in order to reinforce correct spelling and to strengthen students' ability to edit for correct spelling.

CONTINUED

Alice was criticizing all her friends.   She needed a good spanking.

So we all stopped talking to her.   We just ignored her.   Pretty soon she got the point.   She started being nice again.   She knew she needed friendship not just muscles.   So she's winning friends again—and also winning races.

Some correct spellings: **beginning, benefited, coming, criticizing, eating, ended, fatter, getting, happening, hitting, ignored, jogging, jumped, lifted, liked, losing, needed, offering, patted, popping, preferred, running, seemed, spanking, started, stopped, sweating, swimming, talking, thinner, winning**

Extra Write some sentences using words that have suffixes added. Spell some of the words correctly, some incorrectly. Give the sentences to a classmate to edit.

PURPOSE: To review the *y* to *i* rule and to give practice in correcting words to which the rule applies

Before you use this lesson, read the general statement about spelling on page 4. If you go over the *Hints* with the class, tell the students not to worry if they're not sure about what nouns, verbs, and adjectives are. The main spelling problem is adding suffixes to words ending with *y*. Urge students to refer constantly to the correctly spelled words (in bold-faced type) to reinforce correct spelling and to strengthen their ability to edit for correct spelling. It may be useful to do the first sentence of the passage together, and also to read aloud the entire passage so that students will get the meaning of it before they start editing the spelling.

CHANGE y TO i TO ADD es, ed, er, est

The passage below contains many words that end with *y* plus a suffix. Edit the passage to correct the misspellings.

HINT 1: Words that end with *y* with a consonant before it change the *y* to *i* before adding *es, ed, er, est (baby, babies; pity, pitied; easy, easier, easiest).*   **HINT 2:** All words that have a vowel before the *y* just add *s (boy, boys).*

Bob was the happiest, merriest person I ever knew. He told the silliest jokes and the funniest stories. He was friendlier than a litter of puppies.

Bob didn't have any enemies, though some people said he must be the craziest man in town. Why? Because he never worried about anything. He enjoyed everything and always seemed satisfied. He played with babies and bought toys for all the little girls and boys.

All Bob's friends got busier with their duties and didn't take time for fun. But Bob seemed to get happier every day. Some people said they pitied Bob. "Life isn't all parties!" they cried. But I think they envied him, don't you?

Some correct spellings: babies, boys, busier, craziest, cried, duties, enemies, enjoyed, envied, friendlier, funniest, happier, happiest, merriest, parties, pitied, played, puppies, satisfied, silliest, stories, toys, worried

EXTRA Write some sentences or a paragraph using words that end in *y* with suffixes added. Spell some of the words correctly, some incorrectly. Give the sentences or paragraph to a classmate to edit.

PURPOSE: To review the rule for adding suffixes, such as *ness* and *ing,* to words and to give practice in correcting words to which the rule applies

Before you use this lesson, read the general statement about spelling on page 4. Go over the *Hints* if you think your students need them and urge students to refer to the *Hints* instead of just guessing when they are uncertain. Point out the correctly spelled words (in bold-faced type) for reference and reinforcement. Have students learn and copy words they misspell in doing the lesson. It may be helpful to read the entire passage aloud so that students will get the meaning of it before they start editing the spelling.

ADD SUFFIXES

The paragraph below contains many words that end with *y* plus a suffix. It also contains many words that end with consonants plus suffixes. Edit the paragraph to correct the misspellings. After you've edited them, list the words, spelling them correctly.

HINT 1: Words that end with *y* with a consonant before it change the *y* to *i* before adding a suffix *(beauty, beautiful).*   **HINT 2:** However, when you add *ing,* keep the *y (study, studying).*   **HINT 3:** Words that end with consonants don't need any changes *(cheer, cheerful).*   **HINT 4:** Never change a suffix; just add it.

I am always studying people's problems. I can understand bashfulness and clumsiness, but I don't understand meanness. What could be sillier or emptier? Meanness takes all the happiness and merriment out of life. Ignoring mean people is easier than trying to be friends with them. But they are pitiful, really, and we should try to be merciful and helpful. Otherwise they will keep spreading unhappiness.

Some correct spellings: bashfulness, clumsiness, easier, emptier, happiness, helpful, meanness, merciful, merriment, pitiful, sillier, studying, trying, unhappiness

Extra Write some sentences or a paragraph using words that end with *y* with suffixes added. Spell some of the words correctly, some incorrectly. Give the paper to a classmate to edit.

ADD PREFIXES

Some of the prefixes in the passage below are misspelled. You are the editor. Correct the misspelled words either by crossing them out and writing above

~~dissappeared~~ *disappeared*

or by using editor's marks.

dis~~s~~appeared

After you've edited them, list the words, spelling them correctly.

HINT: When you attach a prefix to a word, never change the prefix or the word. Just put them together (*mis + spell = misspell*).

Sally was antissocial. People made her unncomfortable.   She misstrusted and dissliked nearly everyone.   She often wished that everyone would just dissappear.

The reason for Sally's unhappy feelings was that she felt unlloved.   What's more, she felt unnable to make friends.   So she told and reetold herself, "Friends are unimportant."

She hated school.   Whenever she mispelled a word or missread a sentence, she thought everybody was laughing at her.   When she left the room, then rentered, she was sure the children had been talking about her.

One day Sally's teacher said, "Sally, this is nosense.   Your imagination is overrworked.   You make yourself unllovable by thinking that it's true.   So reethink!"

☞

PURPOSE: To review the rule for adding prefixes to root words and to give practice in correcting words to which the rule applies

Before you use this lesson, read the general statement about spelling on page 4. This is a simple rule that helps avoid many errors. Emphasize that prefixes simply get added; there are no changes (prefix + word = correct spelling). Point out the correctly spelled words (in bold-faced type) for reference and reinforcement. Have students learn and copy words they misspell in doing the lesson. It may be helpful to read the entire passage aloud so that students will get the meaning of it before they start editing the spelling.

CONTINUED

Sally's troubles were un~~d~~done by that little talk.   She re~~c~~considered everything.   She decided that she had misunderstood herself and everyone else. From then on, she was unusually friendly.

Some correct spellings: **antisocial, disappear, disliked, misread, misspelled, mistrusted, misunderstood, nonsense, overworked, reconsidered, reentered, rethink, retold, unable, uncomfortable, undone, unhappy, unimportant, unlovable, unloved, unusually**

EXTRA Write a paragraph or several short sentences using many prefix words. Misspell some of the prefix words. Give the paragraph or sentences to a classmate to edit.

PURPOSE: **To review the problems of spelling homonyms correctly and to give practice in editing errors made in using homonyms** *(Editing methods may vary.)*

Before you use this lesson, read the general statement about spelling on page 4. Emphasize that the problem in spelling homonyms usually is not *how* to spell the word but *which* word to spell. Explain and demonstrate the importance of noticing how a word is used in a sentence—in its context. Editors should always keep context in mind. (You may wish to explain that *homonym* comes from the Greek words *homos,* which means "same," and *onyma,* which means "name.") Other troublesome homonyms or near-homonyms are *accept/except, all ready/already, right/write, passed/past, peace/piece, precede/proceed, principal/principle, quiet/quite, stationary/stationery, threw/through, weather/whether.* Whenever you or your students write a homonym, it should be written in a phrase that makes its meaning clear.

SPELLING HOMONYMS CORRECTLY

The passages below contain many misspelled *homonyms.* Homonyms are words that sound the same but that have different meanings:

I <u>hear</u> with my ears.

Come <u>here</u> to me.

Here is a list of very common homonyms that editors need to be aware of:

forth (Bring it *forth* now.)
fourth (third and *fourth*)

its (in *its* place)
it's ("it is") (*It's* here.)

their (*their* gifts)
there (here and *there*)
they're ("they are") (*They're* gone.)

to (go *to* bed)
too (*too* much; me *too*)
two (one, *two*, three)

whose (*Whose* is it?)
who's ("who is") (*Who's* there?)

your (*your* eyes)
you're ("you are") (*You're* a fake.)

Edit the passages below by correcting the misspelled words. Either cross them out and write above

~~whose~~ *who's*

or use editor's marks.

ther*e*

After you've edited them, list the words, spelling them correctly.

HINT: To know which homonym to use, always think what the word means in its sentence.

1. To pigs are to many to have when there both noisy.
2. "Their is entirely two much soup," said the forth person in line. Whose in charge of this restaurant and whose ideas went into its menu? Bring them fourth. Let's see their faces!"
3. Which of your to statues do you think is better? I'd like two see whose face its modeled on.

CONTINUED

4. There fourth child is here in your house. Please hear carefully two ideas she's saying: "Whose always in their helping me with my life and its problems? It's my father and, hear and there, my friends!"

EXTRA   Write some sentences using homonyms; misspell some, correctly spell others. Give your paper to a classmate to edit.

Lesson 23

ie/ei ERRORS

The paragraph below contains twenty-nine words that are spelled with either *ei* or *ie*. Edit the paragraph by writing in the correct letters.

The boy's fr _ie_ nd enjoyed l _ei_ sure.

After you've edited them, list the words, spelling them correctly.

HINT 1: When sound is *ee*, put *i* before *e (field, chief, believe)* except after *c (receive, ceiling)*.
HINT 2: When sound is not *ee*, put *e* before *i (weigh, eight, foreign)*. **HINT 3:** Exceptions are: He *seized (n)either weird leisure*; and his *friend* did *mischief* with a *sieve*.

The n __ ghbor of the f __ rce cash __ r is a fr __ nd of mine. He had a w __ rd problem with ach __ vement tests. He tried work and he tried l __ sure, but n __ ther of them helped. Then he walked through quiet f __ lds before the test. He ate a p __ ce of cake, but he was gr __ ved to find no rel __ f from his ch __ f problem. He thought of becoming a th __ f or wearing a v __ l like a for __ gner. This might sh __ ld him from his n __ ce. She bel __ ved that his brain was __ ther a s __ ve or a counterf __ t. At last he became h __ to a fr __ ght car full of golden s __ ves. They went from floor to c __ ling. He sold these from a p __ r in the harbor, got rich, and became conc __ ted and misch __ vous.

Some correct spellings: **achievement, believed, cashier, ceiling, chief, conceited, counterfeit, either, fields, fierce, foreigner, freight, grieved, heir, leisure, mischievous, neighbor, neither, niece, piece, pier, relief, shield, sieve, sieves, weird**

Extra
Make up an *ie/ei* exercise of your own and give it to a classmate to try.

PURPOSE: **To review the *ie/ei* spelling rule and to give practice in correcting words to which the rule applies**

This is the first of eight lessons on editing spelling errors. Before you begin, read the general statement about spelling on page 4. Note that in this lesson students are given practice only in writing words correctly. This should make them alert to mistakes in their own writing when they edit it. Go over the *Hints*. Note that the *ie/ei* rule is not expressed in the traditional way (Use *i* before *e* except after *c*, or when sounded like *a*, as in *neighbor* and *weigh*.) because it does not cover as many cases. For some pupils it will be useful to do the first two lines of the passage together, explaining why (according to the *Hints*) each word is spelled *ie* or *ei*. Urge students to keep checking the *Hints* and not just to guess. After you check the lesson, have students correct and copy any words they missed.

Lesson 24

FORTY SPELLING DEMONS

The following passage contains forty words that are often misspelled. Twenty-nine of them are misspelled here. Edit the passage. Either cross out the error and correctly write the word above or use editor's marks to correct the error. After you've edited them, list the words, spelling them correctly.

In Febuary the quite doctor surprised evrybody. She gave up medicine. She'd finlly decided to try a diffrent busness. What could she do? The answer, she thoght, was to study grammar and be an editor. That would probly be more intresting than medcine.

She seprated herself from her frends and spent her time amoung books. She spent hours every day in the libary, with usually only ten minits for lunch. It was definitly hard work, but it was necesary. She studied until her head was stuffed with opinons.

At last she was ready. She drove across the country looking for an exellent editing opprtunity. But she didn't suced. She was completly disapointed and embarrassed. Everywhere, people had become sensible and had learned to edit their own writing. Therefore, she changed jobs agan.

Forty demons: **across, again, among, answer, better, business, completely, could, country, decided, definitely, different, disappointed, doctor, embarrassed, excellent, everybody, February, finally, friend, grammar, interesting, library, meant, medicine, minute, necessary, opinion, opportunities, perhaps, probably, quiet, sensible, separate, succeed, surprise, therefore, thought, until, usually**

Extra
Select ten to twenty common words that are difficult for some people in your class to spell. Use them in a paragraph, misspelling some of them. Give the paragraph to a classmate to edit.

PURPOSE: **To review forty troublesome spelling demons and to give practice in editing misspelled demons (*Editing methods may vary.*)**

Before you use this lesson, read the general statement about spelling on page 4. You may explain that there are many more demons than this; a lot of them are included in other spelling-based lessons in this book. Recommend that students keep a list of their own spelling demons, a list that you may wish to check from time to time.

Before attempting the lesson, have students study and try hard to learn the forty demons. Urge them to refer to the list as they do the lesson. Notice that there is a choice of method of correction. The advantage of the cross-out/ write-above method is that it reinforces the correct spelling; the advantage of the editor's mark method is that it alerts students to the particular points of error and how to correct them. It may be helpful to read the entire passage aloud so that students will get the meaning before they start editing the spelling.

PURPOSE: To review the need for the correct punctuation mark at the end of each sentence and to give practice in editing end punctuation *(Answers may vary in choice of periods or exclamation marks.)*

This is a simple, straightforward lesson. Encourage students to read sentences aloud—quietly—to learn to "hear" written sentences. Emphasize that, except in advertising and comic strips, exclamation marks should not be used unless they are clearly needed. Pairs or small groups of students can easily correct this lesson with only minimal help from you. It may be helpful to read the entire passage aloud so that students get the meaning of it before they start editing the punctuation.

Lesson 25   name:

CORRECT PUNCTUATION AT THE ENDS OF SENTENCES

The paragraph below contains twenty sentences. But the editor sees right away that each needs a punctuation mark at the end. You are the editor. Put in the correct punctuation marks.

for a question   ?

for an exclamation   !

for a statement, a request, or a command   ⊙

It is often a matter of judgment whether or not to use an exclamation mark. It depends on what effect you want.

Alicia was thinking about her problems⊙ Why was she doing so poorly in school? Why did she have troubles with writing? Oh, what a miserable life she was leading! She was dying for help with her problems⊙ They simply had to be solved! Then she had an inspiration⊙ Editing, yes, <u>that</u> would do it! Alicia started learning to edit⊙ She learned how to use editor's marks⊙ She even taught them to her best friends⊙ What do you think was the result? Well, I'll tell you⊙ They all got A's in English⊙ How amazing that is! Therefore, students, please learn how to edit⊙ Why not try it? You'll never regret it⊙ It might even help people to communicate better⊙ So, let's go!

EXTRA Write a paragraph that contains question sentences, exclamation sentences, and request, statement, and command sentences. Leave out the punctuation marks at the end of each sentence. Give the paragraph to a classmate to edit.

page 35   YOU ARE THE EDITOR COPYRIGHT © 1981

PURPOSE: To teach students how to "hear" run-ons and to give practice in editing run-ons

It may be helpful to give some practice in listening for the pause and the pitch-drop. Read the directions for the lesson aloud (you may wish to have students assist you in this), emphasizing the pause *and* the pitch-drop at the ends of sentences. Also, read the first two passages aloud before instructing the students to work on the lesson.

Lesson 26   name:

RUN-ON SENTENCES

Run-on sentences are two or more sentences that run together without a period separating them. Sometimes run-on sentences have commas separating them, instead of periods. Punctuate the sentences below so that they don't run on. Start each new sentence with a capital letter and end each one with a period. You can change a comma to a period just by putting a circle around it.

Tom went home⊙ Sally put on her skates⊙

HINT: You can usually "hear" where a sentence should end. As you read aloud, your voice usually pauses and drops in pitch at the end of a sentence. As you edit, it might help you to read the passages very quietly and to listen to what your voice does.

1. the small boy promised never to lie⊙ he forgot how hard truth is⊙

2. a skunk is a cute, cuddly animal⊙ however, the smell is not cuddly⊙ that's why skunks don't get hugged⊙

3. never go near the edge⊙ you might fall in⊙ then you'd really be sorry⊙

4. a teacher pinned a dollar bill under a piece of paper⊙ then he dropped it in the hall⊙ a first grader picked it up and won the No-Litter Prize⊙

5. size is less important than brains⊙ at least that's what my friend thinks⊙ he's four feet tall and weighs fifty-one pounds⊙

6. we think our sun is very large⊙ if it were hollow, it could contain a million earths⊙ however, there are stars in space that could contain half a billion of our suns⊙ there are 100 billion stars in an average galaxy⊙ finally, in the universe there may be 100 million galaxies⊙

EXTRA Write some passages or a paragraph containing run-on sentences. Give your paper to a classmate to edit.

page 36   YOU ARE THE EDITOR COPYRIGHT © 1981

Lesson 27

SENTENCE FRAGMENTS

Below is a paragraph containing several *fragments*. Fragments are pieces of sentences punctuated as if they were complete sentences. By changing the punctuation and capitalization, edit the paragraph so that it has all complete sentences. The first four sentences are done to show you how. Three of the sentences in the paragraph are complete and don't need changing.

You won't need to add or subtract words, but you will need to use editor's marks.

Hint: Read aloud very quietly and listen for groups of words followed by periods that sound as if they need something more to complete them. Combine these groups with other words to make whole sentences.

It was raining hard. When Brian came home from school. Because he had forgotten his raincoat, He was soaked. Even worse, he was freezing cold. What he wanted more than anything else was a bowl of that good hot soup. That his mother often had ready for him. On days like this. But when he opened the door and called upstairs, There was no answer. Where was Mom? Then Brian became aware of soft laughter. Coming from the basement. He grew very scared. He was shivering not only from the cold. But also from terror. Quietly going outside again, Brian yelled for help, Hoping a good neighbor would hear him. And would come to the rescue.

Extra Write a paragraph of your own containing several sentence fragments. Give it to a classmate to edit.

PURPOSE: To review sentence fragments and to give practice in editing them

It may be helpful to reinforce the lesson by reading the passage aloud in a manner that emphasizes fragments and their incomplete sounds. Be sure students understand that a fragment can be edited either by making it into a complete sentence by adding material or (more often) by tying it onto a sentence already in the passage. You may want to remind students of the uses of commas. See the "Writer/Editor's Handbook" (pages 94–95). Then do the first two lines of the passage aloud together before students continue the rest of the lesson on their own. Let students correct their own papers in small groups before you check them. (Encourage the observation that many advertisements are written in sentence fragments and that advertising writers know what they are doing. They are not writing material for school or for business but rather for special effect.)

Lesson 28

COMMAS

The sentences in the paragraph below have the correct punctuation marks at the ends. But the editor sees many sentences that need commas and some that have commas in the wrong places. You are the editor. Put in commas where they are needed:

I like eating and sleeping, but John prefers to starve and read all night.

and take out commas that are not needed:

Lucy, ate a frog.

Hint: Commas show *pauses: I write as well as I can,* (pause) *but editing helps to improve my papers. Yes,* (pause) *my friend stole the elephant.* You almost always pause where two complete sentences are joined by *and, or, but,* and *for.* And you usually pause after *yes, no, however, therefore, for example,* and *well* at the beginnings of sentences. Read the sentences aloud quietly and listen for pauses.

Well, I'm a casual sort of person and I want to let you in on a few secrets of success. First, never get too uptight about your work, see? For example, don't let worry cause you to lose sleep, because that will make you dull the next day. However, don't sleep all the time, friend, or you'll never have a chance to study. Instead, study hard, but then take some time for relaxing, if you get what I mean. To sum it all up, try to achieve the right balance between work and play, for if you don't, you'll be a flop, understand? You understand, but not everybody's that bright!

Write a paragraph of your own that needs editing for commas. Give it to a classmate to edit.

PURPOSE: To review the proper placement of commas and to give practice in editing for commas

Before doing this lesson, it may be helpful to read the entire passage aloud, exaggerating the pauses, before students start editing for commas. After they have done the lesson, correct it as a group by reading the passage aloud—again with some exaggerated pauses. After the basic understanding that a comma usually means a pause is established, students may use some individual editorial judgment in their writing. There is often a choice of whether or not to use commas in certain situations, depending upon the effects a writer wishes to achieve. More commas, for example, can make a sentence read slowly, and also can help create a more formal tone. On the other hand, using fewer commas can help make a sentence fast-paced and can create a more casual tone.

PURPOSE: To review the function of commas to set off introducers and interrupters and to give practice in editing for this function

Many students will be helped by an oral reading of the examples, with the pauses exaggerated. It may be helpful, also, to do the first passage aloud together. Point out that sometimes pauses are very slight or, as with *However* in passage 1, not even there. The same is true after *Listen* in the fifth passage. However, the rules require commas there. But rules for commas in writing are not hard and fast, and often the editor must make a judgment.

COMMAS FOR INTRODUCING AND FOR INTERRUPTING

Words such as *therefore*, and phrases and clauses that introduce a sentence, are usually set off by commas. So are expressions that interrupt the flow of a sentence:

Unfortunately, my dog bit Mike.
Under the apple tree, three mice played and squealed.
Because she is French, her accent is charming.
His name, believe it or not, is Xonx.

HINT: Commas mark pauses. They often come in pairs as in the last example above.

Edit the passages below for commas.

1. Since she can't drive, she always walks. This, as you can see, is hard for an eighty-year-old. However, her son, it seems, doesn't care.

2. Because he's afraid that no one will love him, he eats no fat, I understand. Therefore, he's lost confidence, they say, and needs help.

3. Jim looked, he explained, under the bush and found jewels. Because he's honest, he turned them in and, amazing to say, received a large reward.

4. Although the weather was wet, Ruby, crazy girl, left the house without a coat. Soon it started to snow and sleet. The result, as anyone could have told her, was a bad cold and an absence of seven days, I said <u>seven</u>, from school. It was just before exams, I fear.

5. Listen, you fool, to what I am saying, or else! I mean it, see?

Extra Write some passages of your own that contain a mixture of correct and incorrect uses of commas. Give your paper to a classmate to edit.

PURPOSE: To review the punctuation used with appositives and within a series and to give practice in editing for correct comma usage in these instances

The passage here is thicker with commas than a normal piece of good writing would be. Encourage a class chuckle.

Once this lesson is learned, you may point out that writers differ on whether or not to use a comma before the *and* in a series, unless it is required to make the meaning clear. But you can't go wrong by always using a comma there. Point out also that a one-word appositive is usually not set off (My dog Growly eats parsley.), unless there are pauses (My best friend, Mother, defended me.).

COMMAS USED WITH APPOSITIVES AND IN SERIES

An adjective, as you know, modifies a noun or a pronoun. An *appositive* is a phrase that also modifies a noun or a pronoun. Here's a sentence with an appositive:

Cows, very useful animals, have boring personalities.

In the preceding sentence the phrase *very useful animals* is an appositive. Notice that the phrase has a comma before it and a comma after it. All appositives are set off by commas. (If an appositive comes at the end of a sentence, it has a comma before it and a period after it.) Commas also separate items in series:

Cows are useful, boring, slow, and contented.

Edit the passage below by inserting commas where needed.

Dogs, cats, horses, mice, and hamsters are animals I like. My mother, a woman who always loved animals, had a lot of influence on me, my brother, my seven sisters, and about fifteen cousins. She was passionate about animals, her best friends. In fact, I sometimes wondered if she liked, admired, praised, loved, and even adored them more than her husband, children, brothers, and sisters. However, she had a heart so full of love, affection, warmth, and sympathy that there was room in it for all. Therefore, today, a grown person, I feel lucky that Mother, a true lover of all life, filled me with such warmth, enthusiasm, and sympathy. Now I can adjust to anything, even dogs, cats, horses, and hamsters. That's why people call me Sam, the person who loves you, him, her, them, it, us, everything, everybody, and even myself.

EXTRA Write a passage with appositives and series, but no commas, and give it to a classmate to edit.

Lesson 31

CAPITALIZATION

Read the passage below and find the errors in capitalization. Correct the passage, using the two editor's marks shown at the right. The first sentence of the passage (but not the title) has been edited for you.

≡ /

HINT 1: All sentences should begin with a capital letter. **HINT 2:** Proper names begin with a capital letter (*Robert, Ada Lewis School, India;* but not *my mother, the school, our nation*). **HINT 3:** The first, last, and all major words in a title are capitalized (*"How the Little Boy Is Growing Up"*).

some facts about The world

the Earth is a huge Ball, eight Thousand miles in diameter, Covered with Water, Rock, and Soil. It is surrounded by the Atmosphere, which is about 125 Miles thick, Made up mainly of Nitrogen and Oxygen, and extremely cold at its Outer Edge. At the opposite extreme is the Center of the Earth, the inner core. This Core begins 3,200 Miles below the Surface and is 1,600 Miles in diameter. the Temperature at the Very Center is, perhaps, 9000 degrees fahrenheit. the Circumference of the Earth is about 25,000 Miles, So that if you drove around the Equator at 500 Miles a day, The Trip would take you about seven Weeks. however, you couldn't Drive Because about three-Quarters of the Planet's surface at the Equator is Water.

In fact, the Earth is almost entirely covered with Water. only Thirty Percent is Land. the deepest part of the oceans is named challenger deep. It is in the pacific ocean Southwest of the Island of guam and is

☞

PURPOSE: **To review the rules for capitalization and to give practice in editing capitals**

This is a straightforward lesson giving practice in a much-needed editorial skill in which there is not much room for individual judgment. Emphasize the main point: Special or proper names are capitalized; other words (except titles and sentence beginnings) are not. You might mention that in advertising (not in standard writing) unusual capitalization is used for special effect.

This is a fairly easy lesson for students in pairs or small groups to correct. (Students may miss *Fahrenheit,* which is the thermometric scale named after the German physicist, Gabriel D. Fahrenheit, who developed thermometers that use mercury.)

Lesson 31

CONTINUED

almost Seven Miles deep. the highest Point on the earth is mount everest, which is Almost five and one-half Miles high. the earth Rotates on its Axis once every Twenty-Four hours (one Day), and revolves around the sun at eighteen and one-half Miles per Second. It gets Around once every 365.25 Days, which is called a Year.

how Old is the Earth? It's probably four and one-half Billion Years Old, About sixty million times as Old as You will be when You die, if You live an Average Life of seventy-five Years. that makes You feel pretty Young, Doesn't it? however, You're not too Young to enjoy Reading all about it in a Book called easy Information about The earth and space, by gregory F. shoemaker.

page 118

PURPOSE: To review, further than Lesson 13, the punctuation of direct quotations and to give practice in judging which is better in a given context, direct quotations or indirect quotations *(Answers may vary.)*

Be sure students understand the five *Hints*. Then have the class examine together passages 1 and 2, after which they can do passages 3, 4, and 5. Next, turn them loose on passages 6 and 7, each of which requires some editorial judgment. Finally, discuss the editorial choices and variations. (There is no single best way of writing—even though some parts of some writing are clearly wrong or confusing.)

QUOTATIONS

Often editors see that writing can be made more interesting if it contains *direct quotations*. Direct quotations tell exactly what someone says:

Tom said, "Bob, please fall through the floor."

Indirect quotations tell what someone said but not in the speaker's exact words:

Tom asked Bob to fall through the floor.

Below are five passages of indirect quotations to be edited into direct quotations. The first two have been done for you. You do the next three.

After the five short passages, there are two longer ones. Edit them so that they contain both direct and indirect quotations. When you finish editing, copy all seven passages over in final draft form.

HINT 1: Enclose the words spoken in quotation marks.   HINT 2: Quotation marks almost always appear in pairs, before (") and after (") the spoken material. Commas, periods, question marks and exclamation points that punctuate what is spoken go inside (before) quotation marks at the end.   HINT 3: Use commas to separate all such phrases as *he said, she asked,* and so forth, from the words spoken.   HINT 4: Start the first word spoken with a capital. HINT 5: Start a new paragraph every time there is a new speaker. Now study 1 and 2 below. Notice carefully how the editor used marks to change the passages. Some words were changed, some were deleted, and some were moved. Now edit 3, 4, and 5. Then try 6 and 7.

1. Robert shouted, that Gloria, should drop dead!

2. A man asked President Lincoln, how long a person's legs (should) be! Lincoln replied, that they should be long enough to reach the ground.

3. He asked her, please to be more careful in the future.

4. The teacher told the class, to break up into small groups for discussion of the book. Then John protested, that he hadn't read the book, so how can he could he discuss it?

5. A family was at a restaurant. The waitress asked, how do you they wanted their steaks. The mother said, she wanted

---

CONTINUED

here medium. The father also asked for said medium. However, the son said trustingly, he wanted his large of mine.

6. Mrs. Smith was visiting an art class and saw Sally painting a picture. She asked Sally, what it was is a picture of. Sally replied, that it was is a picture of God. Mrs. Smith then told Sally, that nobody knows what God looks like. Sally looked up and said confidently, that they would will know when she had I have finished the picture.

7. Maria asked said to Ann, to go to the beach with her to see some whales. Ann said, that if there were are whales on the beach, they would will scare all the people away. Maria explained, that the whales weren't aren't on the beach, but they're swimming in the ocean. Ann said she wondered asked, where do they got bathing suits big enough?

Extra   Write a passage about a conversation. Use only indirect quotations. Give it to a classmate to edit by changing some of the indirect quotations to direct quotations.

Lesson 33

HYPHENS AND COLONS

The hyphen (-) has many uses. So does the colon (:). The passages below need to be edited for the correct use of hyphens and colons. The **HINTS** will remind you of some uses of these punctuation marks. When you edit the passages, you'll need to delete some hyphens and colons and add or replace others.

HINT 1: Hyphens are used at the end of a line to indicate that a word has been divided between syllables. Examples: *con-tain, sci-ence, af-ter.* **HINT 2:** Hyphens connect such prefixes as *all, ex,* and *self* to other words (*all-American*). **HINT 3:** Many spelled-out numbers are formed with hyphens (*sixty-one*). **HINT 4:** Colons announce lists (*Bring the following:*). **HINT 5:** Colons follow salutations in business letters (*Dear Ms. Jones:*). **HINT 6:** Colons separate hour and minute (*6:25 P.M.*). **HINT 7:** Colons separate chapter and verse (*Genesis 2:7*).

1. Ex-champion Cooke, a self-made man, now weighs ninety-four pounds. He likes his new job and is at work at 7:30 each day.

2. All-American athlete Robin Coe read from Proverbs 23:12, the following: "Pay attention to your teachers and learn all you can."

3. The letter read thus: "Dear Mom, I'm a self-pitying fool. At 5:30 this morning, exactly forty-two terrible minutes after waking up, I decided to come back home. Love, Jim."

4. Never, never forget your mother, father, and school friends. If you do, you may lead a very unhappy life, and that's too bad.

Extra Write some passages with mistakes in the uses of hyphens and colons and give your paper to a classmate to edit.

YOU ARE THE EDITOR COPYRIGHT © 1981

PURPOSE: To review the rules for the use of hyphens and colons and to give practice in editing for their correct use

Be sure students understand the *Hints.* It may be helpful to write a number of examples of the proper uses of hyphens and colons on the chalkboard for explanation and discussion. You may point out that there are other uses of hyphens not covered in this lesson; refer to your classroom grammar text if you wish to discuss hyphens in more depth.

This lesson may be corrected in small groups or by dictating the correct answers, with the questions dealt with as they arise.

Lesson 34

PRONOUNS

A pronoun is a word used in place of a noun. Many writers misuse pronouns. They may write *I* instead of *me,* or *them* instead of *they,* or *whom* instead of *who.* Edit the sentences below to correct the pronoun usage. You'll need to change some words and edit others.

HINT 1: Pronouns have a subject form: *He is going. Who is there?* **HINT 2:** Pronouns have an object form: *George scolded them* (object of verb). *Give it to Sue and me; I was the one to whom she gave it.* (objects of prepositions). **HINT 3:** The possessive form of a pronoun never uses an apostrophe: *Hers is prettier than theirs or ours.*

1. Don't ask Jack and me who the dog belonged to. It was hers.

2. Whom do you think did that to John and me? Him and I were standing beside Gloria and her. Suddenly Gloria and she hauled off and hit the teacher, John, me, a dog, and them. So it's Gloria and her, that's who. Just ask me!

3. You and I should tell Bob and her about brains. Theirs are better than ours, hers is best of all. She is so smart it gives him and me a pain just to think about it and her. Him and me work so hard, and we get D's. Him and me think marks should be based on all that effort of ours. Who else works so hard? To whom should A's be given? To us!

EXTRA Write some sentences containing lots of pronouns, some wrongly used. Give them to a classmate to edit.

YOU ARE THE EDITOR COPYRIGHT © 1981

PURPOSE: To review the subject, object, and possessive forms of pronouns and to give practice in editing for their correct use

If the *Hint* material is somewhat new to the class, write examples on the chalkboard and explain the uses of subject, object, and possessive forms, both of pronouns and of nouns. Also show that the editor's "ear" can help decide what form the second pronoun should be if the editor mentally cuts out the words before it: She crashed into (the dog and) I. *She crashed into I* simply sounds wrong, so it is clear that the correct form is *me.* Recite a few similar examples so that students get the idea.

PURPOSE: To review the concept of subject-verb agreement and to give practice in editing mistakes in agreement

This lesson is straightforward; the sentences are either right or wrong. The lesson can be corrected in small groups, with a class discussion of questions that arise.

THE AGREEMENT
OF SUBJECT AND VERB

Singular subjects take the singular form of verbs:

One boy runs fast.

Plural subjects take the plural form:

Two boys run fast.

Keep the following passage in the present tense. Edit it so that the subjects and verbs agree. The first two sentences have been done for you.

HINT: Subjects such as one, either, and neither are singular: One of the cows gives milk. Neither of the children likes grits.

Four friends ~~to~~ are camping on a high pass near the Continental Divide. To the east, streams and rain flows to the Atlantic Ocean. To the west, they flow into the Pacific. This thought ~~are~~ is very exciting because not one of the group ~~have~~ has been on the Divide before.

After dinner one night they all does different things. Pat sit by the fire and toast marshmallows. Ann get water from a stream and wash dishes. Irma read a book about wildflowers.

Alice, the strongest, decide to climb a little peak to the north. She ~~have~~ has no trouble reaching the top and look down on her friends. They is are now crawling into their sleeping bags. She begin to feel the cold sunset wind that blows out of the west. She decide to run back to camp. At first all the paths is are easy to

CONTINUED

find, but then she realize that one of the turns ~~were~~ was wrong. She is in a strange place. She have heard about people who panics when they gets lost like this, and she start to shiver. Both fear and cold causes her to tremble. But finally she finds the right path and rejoin her friends just before dark.

EXTRA Write a passage in which some subjects and verbs do not agree. Give it to a classmate to edit.

name:

THE TENSE OF VERBS

Edit the following passages so that the tense of the verbs is correct. *Tense* comes from a Latin word meaning "time." Basically there are three tenses: past, present, and future. Unless there is a reason to change, all verbs in a passage should be of the same tense.

Here's an example of mixed tenses. Notice how the sentence reads before and after editing:

At 6:05, John will go to see his dog; at 6:10 he *will* petted him; and at 6:15 he *will* feeds him.

The sentence was edited from future, past, and present tenses to *all future*. Often, however, there *is* a reason for changing tense: *He left yesterday (past), but tomorrow he will stay (future).*

1. There *are* ~~were~~ three tenses in language, and they *are* ~~will be~~ past, present, and future. One of the troubles I ~~will~~ always have *is* ~~was~~ keeping to the same tense. Reading this, you *can see* ~~could have seen~~, I still ha*ve* the trouble. Maybe tomorrow Miss Smith *will* finally teache*s* me.

2. "I came, I *saw* ~~will see~~, I conquer*ed*." That's what the famous Julius Caesar ~~will say~~ *said* when he ~~was~~ defeat*ed* his enemy. The three short statements ~~will~~ say a lot.

3. An eight-year-old girl ~~will~~ show*ed* her artwork to a visitor, and the visitor compliment*ed* her on an excellent drawing of a dog. The girl sa*id* ~~says~~, "I really can't draw a dog, so when I ~~will~~ have to draw a dog, I ~~was~~ *was* drawing a horse, and it ~~will~~ come*s* out looking like a dog." "My!" the visitor ~~will say~~ *said*, "how cute!"

4. Yesterday, he ~~will think~~ *thought* how good he fe*lt*, and he laugh*ed*.

EXTRA Write a passage entirely in the present tense and give it to a classmate to edit into entirely past tense, or the other way around.

PURPOSE: To review the concept of tense and to give practice in editing for tense *(Answers may vary.)*

Several different editings of these passages will likely result. For example, the sentence in the directions could be cast entirely in the past tense ("John went to see his dog; . . ."). Explain this and emphasize that writers should know what tense they're starting with and should stick with it unless there's a reason to change. It may be helpful to have students do the first passage and then go over it in class before the rest of the lesson is completed. Emphasize that it will be helpful to read over each passage before starting to edit it. This is a good lesson to correct together in class, showing that there is latitude for differences in editorial judgment.

---

name:

THE BUSINESS LETTER

Edit the business letter below for punctuation and capitalization.

HINT 1: In addresses, use commas to separate the town from the state but not the state from the zip code (Dallas, TX 75217). **HINT 2:** In dates, use a comma to separate the month and day from the year (June 20, 1984). **HINT 3:** Start the words in the salutation with a capital letter; use a colon (:) after them (Dear Dr. Fox:). **HINT 4:** Begin the first word in the formal close with a capital letter, but use small letters for the other words. End with a comma (Very truly yours,).

6337 Gravers Avenue
Smithfield, NJ 07703
May 31, 1983

Mr. Gerald F. Crowd
Youth employment Division, Yankee Clothes Co.
1732 Pine street
Baton rouge, LA 70805

Dear Mr. crowd:

Thank you for your letter. I expect to be in Baton rouge on june 9. I shall be very glad to see you then, at 9:45 A.M.

sincerely yours,

Oswald O. newbold

Extra Write a business letter than needs editing for capitalization and punctuation. Give it to a classmate to edit.

PURPOSE: To review the mechanics of business letters and to give practice in editing a business letter

When this lesson is finished and corrected, it may be helpful to reinforce it by having several students write short business letters on the chalkboard for class editing. Point out that in business, straightforwardness and correctness generally pay dividends.

PURPOSE: To review and test students' ability to edit punctuation and capitalization

This is a good lesson to use as a review of the earlier lessons on editing punctuation and capitalization. It may be helpful to read the entire passage aloud so that students will get the meaning of it before they start editing. If you wish, this lesson can be used as a test; however, its most important function is to review, to reinforce, and to give practice in editing. Remind the class that paragraphing is also a form of punctuation. For many students the final copying of the passage will not be necessary.

PUNCTUATION AND CAPITALIZATION REVIEW

The following story has correct spelling and paragraphing, but it contains many errors in punctuation and capitalization. Use your knowledge and editor's marks to correct the mistakes. Take your time and work carefully. There are about 125 corrections needed. When you've finished editing the story, copy it in final-draft form on another sheet of paper.

The secret Intelligence of dogs

most people think That dogs are less intelligent than Human Beings. I know otherwise dogs just act less Bright in fact dogs minds are much Better than peoples. Theyre just too bright to act bright. this conversation in Our House will prove it I think

My Mother looks very worried. She says to me, "I'm so stupid I didn't Get any bitty-bits for fido."

Fido replies cheerfully With a wagging tail, "Woof! Woof! I am unhappy. I say to mom, "but we Just cant let fido starve!

Fido gets up and licks my hand And says "Woof! Arf!

Well," Groans Mom, "i've got to get your little Sister from her music lesson. youll just have to climb on your bike And ride to the store For some bitty-bits." "but mom I've got a lot of Editing Homework to do," I moan.

Fido says Arf! Arf! and licks My hand.

CONTINUED

Go! says Mom. "Never mind the editing first things first

So what do you think happens? Ill tell you what happens. Fido woofs a few more times And lies down with a happy sigh To go to sleep. Meanwhile however I get on my bike and risking failure in editing Ride three Miles to the store.

when I get back Fido is just waking up from his nap he wags his tail, arfs cheerfully And gets his Blasted Bitty-Bits. my Mother comes back with my Sister Then my Father comes in late and angry From teaching school and marking papers.

Dogs are so dumb" says my Sister When she hears the story. People are dumber I say, and I go off miserably Passing Fido who is well fed And looking as if he is asleep on the soft living room Rug. When nobody is looking He winks at our cat Who smiles back.

page 123

WORD ORDER IN SENTENCES I

Up pick please eggs those you were enough

clumsy to drop John on the floor, please.

Nobody would ever write a sentence like that, but here's the way an editor might straighten it out using circles, arrows, and editor's marks:

Up pick please eggs those you were enough

clumsy to drop John on the floor, please.

The edited sentence reads: John, please pick up those eggs you were clumsy enough to drop on the floor.

Here's another example. Notice that the editor has added the word *for* but has not changed the meaning of the sentence.

ORIGINAL:

We threw the horse over the fence some hay.

EDITED:

We threw *for* the horse over the fence some hay.

The edited sentence reads: We threw some hay over the fence for the horse.

Edit the following sentences so that they say what you think the writer meant them to say. You may add, change, or subtract a word or two, but don't change any ideas. When you have finished editing, copy the sentences in final-draft form on another sheet of paper.

1. All students should study before watching TV two hours a night if they want to do well in school.

2. Please send me instructions how for to make health bread in the enclosed envelope, please.

3. There's a not finer city police chief than Joe O'Malley in the country according to experts.

PURPOSE: To teach how to edit the order of words in a sentence and how this will clarify the sentence's meaning *(Answers may vary.)*

Many students will be helped by your discussing the purpose of the lesson. Explain that sentences we speak often sound sensible despite mistakes because of pauses and emphasis, but in *writing* there is no unmistakably heard voice. Word order and punctuation, therefore, are crucial. For instance, in the second example, if the words "We threw the horse over the fence" are spoken very rapidly and there is a strong pause before "some hay," the sentence almost makes sense. But it is a comic disaster when read silently. Try it out yourself first, then share the experience with your students.

It may be a good idea to have the class do passage 1 as a group, with you writing on the chalkboard, before students work on the rest of the sentences independently.

CONTINUED

4. Your idea will be considered by the principal for solving the lateness problem.

5. Jill scolded the boy who disapproved of his actions.

6. When I tried I got scratched to remove the cat's bowl.

7. Marlene sent the suits to the cleaners that were dirty as a favor to her father.

8. Chris found the boy who had lost his way with the help of the Girl Scouts.

9. Ann fed the child who didn't want her to go hungry.

10. Mr. Toll's influence was great and admired much on his students by all the parents.

EXTRA There are seven places where *only* can be placed in the sentence below. Each placement gives the sentence a different meaning. Draw arrows from *only* to each place and number each arrow. Be prepared to read the seven different versions aloud and to explain the meaning of each.

only

She scolded the little child last week.

PURPOSE: **To teach and give practice in using editor's marks to change word order (Editing methods and answers may vary.)**

Explain that no one would ever write sentences as scrambled as these are. The purpose here is to show how to edit word order, so have fun! In some sentences, there is more than one possibility for intelligent reordering. Discussing these will help students appreciate the flexibility of our language—and the many ways that this flexibility allows us to go wrong. Further, point out to students that in some instances they have the choice of using either circles and arrows or transpose marks. The best way to correct the lesson is to have a few students write their edits on the chalkboard for discussion, or to discuss them in small groups.

WORD ORDER IN SENTENCES II

Editors often change the order of words in sentences to make the meaning clear. Sometimes they edit just to make a sentence sound better. To do this, they use circles, arrows, transpose marks, and other editor's marks.

ORIGINAL:

The river we ate our picnic down by.

EDITED:

(The river) we ate our picnic down by.

The edited sentence reads: We ate our picnic down by the river.
Edit the sentences below. Use circles, arrows, transpose marks, and, when you need them, other editor's marks.

1. Please under the table go.
2. Very nice to all of us my mother is.
3. I simply why you do it cannot understand.
4. Josh really my best friend, is quite bright.
5. Look the table under and find some money you will.
6. Circles and arrows use to put in order words.
7. Our teacher harder works than the students do.
8. Never again please, do that to me.
9. Then she laughed aloud and first Molly quietly giggled.
10. To read books in the library is a very good place.

Extra Write some sentences in which the word order sounds wrong or makes the meaning unclear. First, try editing them yourself to be sure it can be done. Then give the unedited sentences to a classmate to edit. Check later to see if you both edited them the same way.

PURPOSE: **To review the problem and sound of transition from idea to idea and to give practice in editing for good transition (Answers may vary.)**

There are no single right answers to these passages. For example, the edited passage could also be done: Because our dog barks but doesn't bite, she's useful but harmless. Encourage students to use their ears and brains to edit passages into smoothly progressing order. Discuss the various answers. The object is not a single correct version but rather an understanding of the various ways to edit for good transition. You may want to do the first passage with the whole class, discussing various possibilities, and then read aloud a good version to further demonstrate how transitions work.

TRANSITIONS

Each of the four passages below contains two or more ideas. However, the writers have failed to take the reader smoothly from one idea to the next. Moving from one idea to the next is called *transition*. Edit each passage to ensure good transitions. If necessary, you may combine sentences and add words. This passage has been edited to show you how:

Our dog barks, but she doesn't bite. Therefore, She's useful but harmless.

HINT: Some transition words you may use are: *although, and, but, even though, furthermore, however, nevertheless, on the other hand, since, so, thus, while.*

1. My mother is strong, forceful, and loud. While My father is tender, cooperative, and quiet. However, I love them both, and I hope they don't change.

2. A tough math course may be good for very able students, but Molly knows a boy who broke under the strain of such a course.

3. Knowing how to spell is an advantage in life. even though Good spelling has no connection with high intelligence, and Most misspelled words are perfectly easy to understand.

4. In February, our new car began to rust. Because There was a lot of snow and ice. The roads were heavily salted. However, When we moved to Alabama the rusting stopped. Nevertheless, I prefer the North, because I love to ski. Therefore, I choose rust holes and skiing over good paint and no snow.

EXTRA Write some passages containing ideas that need connecting. Give them to a classmate to edit for smooth, sensible transitions.

Lesson 42

name:

DIRECTIONS

Directions for drawing the diagram below should be clear enough that someone could draw the diagram just as it is without having seen it.

One inch
H S I F

Edit the following directions so that they are clear. Remember to be exact. For example, in the first line of the passage, delete the word *figure* and replace it with the word *rectangle*. You will need to change many words and add many more.

Draw a ~~figure~~ *rectangle* ~~several~~ *four* inches long and one inch high, lying ~~down~~ *on its long side. With dotted lines* Divide the ~~figure~~ *rectangle* into four ~~parts~~ *equal squares*. At the bottom ~~of one part~~ draw an inch. In the next square to the right, draw a spiral curving clockwise from the center, ~~part make a curved line going round and round~~ *filling most of the square*. ~~Then~~ *In the next square to the right,* make a ~~medium-sized~~ *half-inch* circle with a little x in the center. ~~In the center of the last square,~~ ~~Finally~~ draw a ~~square in the last part~~ *half-inch square and at the center of the rectangle Label the inch.* Below ~~the figure~~ print ~~four letters that~~ *the word fish in capital letters and spell a word backwards.*

EXTRA Draw a simple diagram. Write unclear, inexact directions for reproducing it. Give the directions to a classmate to edit. OR: Write inexact, unclear directions for performing an action like tying a shoe, scrambling an egg, or making a telephone call. Give the directions to a classmate to edit.

PURPOSE: **To review clarity and completeness in writing directions and to give practice in editing directions** *(Answers may vary.)*

This lesson could prove frustrating to students of lesser ability. The answer key presents one possible editing; it's not the only correct one. When students are finished editing, go over the exercise carefully, sentence by sentence, with the entire group, asking for various student versions. Emphasize the need for specific information in giving directions.

Lesson 43

name:

DESCRIPTIONS

To describe something well you must use specific words to give important details. For example, "The meal was awful," is not a very good description. A more exact description might say, "The soup was ice cold, the bread was as hard as a hockey puck, and the meat loaf tasted like newspaper."

Below is a picture of a sentence machine and a description of the machine. Edit the description to make it clear, accurate, and complete. You will need to change many words and add many more. Remember your editor's marks. After you've finished editing, copy the description over in final-draft form on a separate sheet of paper.

The sentence machine ~~is old and made of metal~~ *was made of cast iron around 1890.* It is ~~fairly large~~ *nearly twice as tall as a person;* it stands on ~~legs~~ *four legs,* and its main part is a ~~sort of bowl~~ *large, round bowl bigger at the bottom than at the top.* Above the bowl hang two containers, ~~similar to funnels. The container on the left~~ One is full of ~~parts of~~ *capital letters* sentences and the ~~other~~ *one on the right is* full of ~~other parts~~ *punctuation marks and spaces.* When a person ~~runs~~ *turns the crank on the left funnel* the machine, ~~one container~~ drops *letters* into the ~~main part~~ *big bowl;* and the ~~other~~ *right* one drops ~~other stuff~~ *the punctuation and spaces.* An opening ~~on one side~~ *at the bottom right of the bowl* has sentences coming out of it *saying, "I make sentences! Yes, I really do."* ~~telling what the machine does.~~

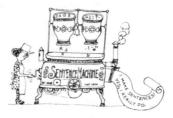

EXTRA Draw or find a picture of a fairly simple object. Write a description of it that isn't very accurate. Give the picture and your paper to a classmate to edit.

PURPOSE: **To review the necessity for clarity and completeness in writing descriptions and to practice editing for such** *(Answers may vary.)*

As with Lesson 42, this is a difficult lesson that may prove frustrating and discouraging to students of lesser ability. Use the suggested editing in the answer key as a guide. When students are finished editing, go over the lesson, sentence by sentence, with the entire group, asking for various student versions. Emphasize the importance of giving specific details.

PURPOSE: To review the order of ideas in paragraphs and to give practice in editing for order (Answers may vary.)

This is a hard lesson; but if it were not hard, it would not be realistic. The best way to start work on each paragraph is to look for a possible topic sentence and number it *1*. Suggest that students keep numbering and renumbering the sentences, all the time mumbling the sentences aloud, until they've got the best order. It may be a struggle, but so too is clear thinking. Don't hurry the lesson. Encourage those who feel confused simply to do their best. They are thinking about a very important matter: logical order. Correct the lesson by reading aloud, slowly and clearly, the suggested correct editings. Allow discussion of variations that may also work.

Lesson 44 — name:

THE ORDER OF SENTENCES IN PARAGRAPHS

Editors try to make sure that ideas are written in a sensible order. In each of the five paragraphs below, the sentences are out of order. Edit the order of the sentences by writing the number *1* at the start of what should be the first sentence, the number *2* at the start of the second sentence, and so forth. Use a pencil so that you can erase if you change your mind. When you're done, read aloud (quietly) your reordered version. If need be, edit some more. Then copy the final version on a separate sheet of paper. In passage 1, the first sentence has been numbered for you. In passage 3, the first and last sentences have been numbered.

HINT: Each of these paragraphs should begin with a *topic sentence* that states the general idea of the paragraph.

(2) 1. I've eaten dozens and enjoyed every one. (3) The main dish is always hot and well seasoned. (5) Finally, the dessert is rich and tasty. (1) I don't agree with people who complain about airplane meals. (6) Therefore, give me an airplane meal over home cooking any day! (4) The salad is always cold, crisp, and full of fresh vegetables.

(2) 2. First, older people are respected and helped. (3) They are treated with good humor and kindness. (7) Further, the young are bossed around by everybody. (4) Also, the elderly have beautiful memories to comfort them in troubled times. (1) Let me explain why I'd much rather be old than young. (5) On the other hand, the young have to worry about the future. (6) Hardly anybody respects youthfulness anymore, and youngsters have to do all the work. (8) That's why I hope to grow old fast and stay old long.

Lesson 44 — name:

CONTINUED

(2) 3. First, good spelling usually makes a good impression on other people, and misspelling makes a bad impression. (4) Second, it is a sad fact that many people think that poor spellers are stupid. (3) If you make a good impression, you are likely to do better in almost every way. (5) Lots of good spellers aren't always bright, and many poor spellers are quite bright. (6) But that doesn't seem to change what so many people think. (8) So, if you want the best chance to be accepted and to get a job, work on your spelling. (7) And if people think you're stupid, they are less likely to hire you for a job. (1) Unfortunately, knowing how to spell correctly is an important advantage in life.

(4) 4. The sounds of the radio also keep my own thoughts from turning bad and making me feel very low. (2) The music and talk that come out of it comfort me. (3) These sounds shut me off from all the trouble of the nasty world. (1) Wherever I go, I like to have my portable radio with me, turned on loud. (7) If people knew, they'd get a radio too; then we'd all be happy and nobody would hurt anybody. (6) They just don't know what my beautiful radio is saving me from. (5) Therefore, when people on buses and city streets give me dirty looks, I ignore them.

Extra Write a simple, carefully ordered paragraph. Begin it with a topic sentence. Then rewrite it so that two or more sentences are out of order. Give it to a classmate to edit.

Lesson 45

THE ORDER OF PARAGRAPHS IN A PAPER

Editors read long papers carefully to see that the ideas are arranged in a way that makes good sense. Usually, the main ideas are organized into paragraphs. It's important to have the paragraphs in the best possible order.

Here are five topics for paragraphs on the subject, "The Usefulness of Earthworms." Edit the topics into good order by numbering the five blanks 1 through 5.

The Usefulness of Earthworms

_2_ how earthworms help plants grow

_1_ what earthworms are

_4_ how earthworms help us catch fish

_5_ summary of why we should be thankful for earthworms

_3_ how earthworms are useful to birds

Many paragraphs begin with a topic sentence that suggests the main idea of the paragraph. Here are five topic sentences for five different paragraphs. Put them into the best order by numbering the five blanks 1 through 5.

Exercise Is Good for You

_4_ Of course, you should not overdo exercise.

_3_ So you see, most people who exercise live longer and feel better.

_1_ Most people don't get enough exercise.

_2_ Exercise benefits not only the body but also the mind.

_5_ Here are some kinds of exercises that are good for you.

page 61   YOU ARE THE EDITOR COPYRIGHT © 1981

PURPOSE: To review the order of main ideas in a longer paper and to give practice in editing for order *(Answers may vary.)*

After students have read and understood the directions, have them do the earthworm exercise, and then correct and discuss it. Point out that the first and last sentences are firmly established, but the correct order of the middle sentences is arguable. Note the difference between *topics* in the first passage and *topic sentences* in the second two passages. Also remind students that the items are not complete paragraphs, only topics or topic sentences to be turned into paragraphs. The main object of this lesson is to edit for order not to decide which single order is correct. All-class or small-group discussion will be enlightening.

If students find this lesson difficult, try doing each part of it aloud, as a discussion. Or, you may want to do the lesson yourself, thinking aloud and explaining your choices, so that students can eavesdrop on the process. Also, small-group discussion of ordering should work well.

When students finish the lesson, read the answers aloud and discuss them. Note variations that also work.

Lesson 45

CONTINUED

Here are the topic sentences of the paragraphs in a longer paper. Edit the order of the paragraphs by numbering them 1 through 10.

TV Is Bad for Your Education

_7_ Further, the tube can cut you off almost entirely from books and homework.

_8_ I'll admit, however, that some programs are educational.

_1_ The average American has watched 18,000 hours of TV before graduating from high school.

_6_ Obviously, it's important to stop and think and discuss if one is to do well in school.

_3_ Thus, watching TV becomes a habit long before the child starts school.

_2_ One reason for the trouble is that too many parents want their kids to be quiet and to stay out of the way.

_4_ A part of the problem is that parents, too, are TV addicts.

_5_ What, then, are the effects on the mind of the TV addict?

_9_ But what you can learn from TV doesn't make up for the harm too much watching causes.

_10_ To summarize, I'll state seven key words that prove the case.

Extra Make up ten topic sentences for an out-of-order paper and give them to a classmate to put into order. The easiest way is to write them in the right order first, then scramble them.

page 62   YOU ARE THE EDITOR COPYRIGHT © 1981

page 128

PURPOSE: **To review how parts of an outline translate into paragraphs and to give practice in editing for paragraphing**

Have students read the directions and study the outline. Then, before they do the lesson, ask students how many paragraphs the outline will require (four). Caution against too many short paragraphs. It may be helpful to read aloud the first several lines of the passage and to discuss where paragraphs ought to occur. Encourage students to keep referring to the outline.

You may mention that if the paper were much longer and more complete, each subtopic (A, B, C) might make a paragraph; but this is not so in this short paper. In short papers, as in most writing, deciding where to start a paragraph requires careful judgment.

PARAGRAPHING IN A PASSAGE

At the right is the beginning of an outline for an essay on the topic, "Marks: Good or Bad?" Below is the first part of an essay written on the basis of the outline. The passage should contain four paragraphs, but the writer has used poor judgment. Show where you think new paragraphs should begin:

¶

and where there should be no new paragraphs:

〰 (run in)

To help you, the first two marks have been made.

OUTLINE

I. Introduction: the problem

II. What marks are
   A. Letter systems
   B. Number systems

III. Arguments in favor of marks
   A. Give definite information
   B. Motivate students to study
   C. Needed as records

IV. Arguments against marks
   A. Schoolwork too complicated to be marked
   B. Cause harmful competition
   C. Cause pressure, cheating

Marks: Good or Bad?

Should schools give marks or not? Some parents, teachers, and even students like marks and demand that schools give them. Others feel that marks are harmful in many ways. ¶ Before we go further, let's look at the two main marking systems. One system uses letter grades: 〰 A, B, C, D, and F— A meaning "excellent" and F meaning "failure." Another common system uses numbers, usually from below 60 to 100. <u>Below 60</u> means "failure"; <u>90 and above</u> means "excellent." ☞

CONTINUED

Now, what are the main arguments in favor of marks? 〰 First, they give information about how well a student is doing. Second, marks make students work. 〰 They make students study harder. Third, marks are needed for records so that teachers in the next grade can know what each student needs. 〰 Also, when students change schools, the new school will have records to help put each student in the right class. ¶ The arguments against marks are quite strong too. The first is that schoolwork is very complicated. 〰 Therefore, a simple mark isn't enough to describe all the work students do in a subject. Further, marks cause students to compete with each other in harmful ways. Third, 〰 If students are marked, they are likely to feel great pressure from classmates and from home. 〰 This will cause some of them to cheat, and that doesn't help learning at all.

EXTRA Write an outline and then write a well-organized essay based on the outline. Copy it over, with mistakes in paragraphing, and give the copy to a classmate to edit.

Lesson 49

name:

BEGINNINGS

Some writers have problems beginning their stories or essays. Sometimes they start too fast and don't give enough information. This kind of beginning can confuse the reader, who may have trouble understanding what is happening. More often, writers begin too slowly, writing much more than they need to. This kind of beginning is usually boring to the reader.

Look at the beginnings below. If they need improvement, edit them. You may delete words or even whole sentences; you may add words and sentences. You may replace poor words with better ones. If you think any of the beginnings are good as they stand, mark them OK. The first beginning is edited for you to suggest how to go about the task.

HINT 1: Don't say, "I'm going to write about . . ."—just write. **HINT 2:** Sometimes it works well to begin with a strong statement or question that will arouse the reader's interest.

1. ~~I want to tell you about a very interesting thing~~ that happened to me a few days ago. ~~It has to do with~~ my courageous cat and a very fierce, cowardly dog. ~~They~~ met on the way to the same trash can.

2. ~~Seeing as I am not an authority on this subject, I shall write on another.~~ ~~What I know most about is~~ fish. ~~They~~ fascinate me, totally.

OK 3. What better way to get someone to change her mind than to face her with facts? That's what Bob did after lunch when he met Sue.

4. ~~For breakfast on Saturday morning we had~~ ~~orange juice, blueberry pancakes, syrup, milk, and all~~ ~~the raisins we wanted to fill us up.~~ Saturday was the day of the donkey race, and Friday night my donkey Crumbles had been even more stubborn than usual. So this morning I was worried. Crumbles, though, didn't

---

Lesson 49

name:

CONTINUED

have a worry in the world. ~~I sometimes think I worry~~ ~~too much.~~ She was grazing quietly in the pasture, and her calmness made me angry. ~~She likes breakfast too,~~ ~~even though it's only hay.~~ "Well, Crum," I said, "this is your day—or else!"

5. ~~I got the facts for this paper from the following~~ ~~books: The Remarkable Firefly, The Wonders of~~ ~~Lightning Bugs, and How Fireflies Work. First let me~~ ~~tell you some facts I think you will like.~~ The fire of a firefly is caused by five chemicals in its belly. When these are set off by a sixth chemical, the firefly lights up. And why? Flashing light is the way male fireflies find females. ~~Isn't that interesting?~~

OK 6. I have no trouble getting along with people. It's ghosts who cause all my problems. If you think this means I'm crazy, you may be right, but let me tell you about it first.

7. Teaching school is not nearly as easy as some pupils seem to think it is. ~~It really is too bad that~~ ~~people can't try harder to be helpful to each other.~~ ~~That would make teaching school easier.~~ It took teacher James Drick three periods of his first day on his first job to find that out. The problem wasn't his personality or bad students, but something else.

EXTRA Write a couple of good beginnings of papers and a couple of poor ones. Without saying which are which, give them to a classmate to edit.

PURPOSE: **To stimulate thinking about how best to begin papers and to give practice in editing beginnings (Answers may vary.)**

Point out that time spent on writing a good beginning for a paper is time well spent. After students have read the directions, go over aloud the "before" and "after" versions of the first passage. There's lots of room for differences of opinion about these items. Discuss; don't insist. The object of this lesson is to make students conscious of how they start their papers and aware of the rich variety of possibilities available to editor and writer.

PURPOSE: To teach students to address their readers when they write and to edit their writing appropriately—both for the readers and for the writer's own purpose (Answers may vary.)

After the directions are understood, examine and discuss the "before" and "after" versions of the edited example. The best way to deal with this lesson when it is finished is to discuss the edits in small groups or with the entire class. There are no correct answers, but there are very good ones and very bad ones. You may wish to select some good ones and use them for discussion. You can also, for discussion's sake, read aloud the suggestions in the answer key.

WORDS AND TONE TO SUIT READERS AND PURPOSE

Editors sometimes notice that writers use words and groups of words that don't sound right for their readers. Edit the passages below by deleting words or phrases that you think don't suit the readers. (Look up the words you don't know in a dictionary.) Some deleted words will have to be replaced. Here's an example.

Mrs. Reed's chalkboard note to seventh graders:
Dear ~~children~~ *students*: Hurry to your seats ~~like nice little people~~. We have ~~such~~ an exciting ~~little~~ game to play if you all ~~are very good little people~~ *can keep quiet*. ~~Your loving teacher~~ Thank you. —Mrs. Reed

1. **Principal Gray to students:** *Notices:* ~~Warning!~~ Any ~~student brat~~ ~~in this joint~~ found ~~masticating~~ *chewing* gum *in school* will be required to ~~make a visitation to my administrative headquarters~~ *see me in my office*. ~~Charles Gray, Principal~~ ~~Charlie G., Your pal~~

2. **Fire drill notice in fifth-grade homeroom:**
Attention! ~~Requested!!!!~~ In case of ~~conflagration~~ *fire*, ~~duly~~ ~~proceed~~ *walk* down the main corridor to the second red-colored door, turn ~~to your~~ left ~~(not right)~~, *and go* ~~descend~~ *down* the stairway ~~and continue~~ *walking* along quietly to the ~~automobile~~ *parking* lot, all the while ~~paying~~ attention to special directions.

3. **Request to parents from eighth-graders:**
Dear ~~Mommies and Daddies~~ *Parents*: We ~~would just love to have~~ *need* your help for our ~~nifty little class~~ play ~~get it? We~~. ~~implore you to~~ *Please* share with us ~~kiddies~~ any articles of clothing that ~~could~~ *we* ~~be employed~~ *use* as costumes for

page 69   YOU ARE THE EDITOR COPYRIGHT © 1981

CONTINUED

pirates. ~~Oh dear, we forgot to inform you that~~ our ~~dramatization~~ *play* is ~~entitled~~ *called* Watch Out for Pirates! ~~Your Loved Ones~~ *Thank you — The Eighth Grade*

4. **Space-war action in an adventure book:** The invading aliens didn't move at first. ~~But~~ then they began to ~~go~~ *creep* slowly toward the people. When they got *closer* ~~nearby~~ they ~~moved very rapidly~~ *rushed* forward.
Marsha ~~spoke to them~~ *screamed* "Stop!" But she could tell they weren't going to ~~discontinue~~ *stop*.
Then a man ~~said at the top of his voice~~ *shouted*, "~~End the lives of~~ *Kill* them all! ~~Assassinate~~ *Kill* these aliens and we'll ~~move rapidly to~~ *rush* their ship!"
Marsha ~~revolved~~ *turned* to see who had ~~spoken loudly~~ *shouted*. It was the ~~person~~ *man* whose sister had been ~~made very uncomfortable~~ *tortured*. Then some ~~of the~~ people began to ~~use their guns~~ *shoot*. The aliens ~~leaned down~~ *fell* under the laser fire. ~~Oh, boy, how exciting it was!~~ Then all ~~became noiseless~~ *was quiet*.

5. **Note from teacher inviting Mr. Jones, the principal, to visit a class:** *Dear Mr. Jones:* ~~Oh Principal!~~ My fifth-grade ~~darlings~~ *are* ~~are laying a lot of~~ *causing me* trouble ~~on me~~. Please, ~~oh please~~ when you've nothing better to do ~~get yourself down here to take in the scene~~ *have the time, pay a visit to the class*. ~~Yours truly~~ I would be ~~extravagantly~~ *very* grateful for your ~~aid and assistance~~ *help*. —Mr. Fred ~~R.~~ Ponderous

EXTRA Write passages that sound wrong for the intended readers. Give them to a classmate to edit. Be sure to tell who the readers are.

page 70   YOU ARE THE EDITOR COPYRIGHT © 1981

Lesson 51

name:

EXACT WORDS

Editors know how to change dull, inexact words and phrases to interesting, exact ones. For example:

A playground: ~~The girl went~~ up the ~~thing.~~
Maxine scrambled clumsily *jungle gym*

Examine the eight sentences below. Delete the underlined words or phrases and replace them with better words or phrases. (You may need to delete or change some words that aren't underlined.)

1. **At a fire:** The ~~man went~~ into the ~~building.~~
   chief rushed *church.*
2. **At the zoo:** A ~~person spoke to~~ an ~~animal.~~
   child snorted at *ape.*
3. **At a swimming pool:** ~~Four girls went~~ under a
   Judy, Joy, Jane, and Jo dove
   ~~floating object~~ and ~~came up~~ beside ~~someone~~ who
   plastic duck *surfaced* *Josh*
   ~~made a noise.~~
   sneezed.
4. **At the airport:** ~~Some things passed by~~ the ~~place~~
   Three private jets flew over *hangar*
   while ~~she~~ was ~~standing there.~~
   Mary *working on her plane.*
5. **A thank-you note:** I was ~~glad~~ to have the ~~gift,~~ and
   thrilled *watch*
   you are very ~~kind~~ to give me ~~something~~ so ~~nice.~~
   generous *jewelry* *beautiful.*
6. **A description:** The ~~dog~~ was ~~big~~ and ~~made a terrible~~
   greyhound *long and sleek*
   ~~noise.~~
   growled fiercely.
7. **A dream:** The red ~~car~~ was ~~moving~~ toward me, and I
   convertible *speeding*
   ~~was~~ on the edge of ~~high place~~ holding onto my ~~toy.~~
   stood *a cliff* *water pistol.*
8. **In a kitchen:** He ~~cooked meat,~~ ~~cooked vegetables,~~
   George fried steaks, boiled carrots,
   and ~~made dessert.~~
   baked cookies.

EXTRA Write a passage with lots of dull words in it and give it to a classmate to edit.

PURPOSE: To review the strength of specific words and to give practice in editing vague words into specific words (*Answers will vary.*)

Allow the class to suggest other ways to edit the playground example and also, perhaps, various possibilities for passage 1. Edits will vary, and each answer suggested is only one possibility out of many. There will be great value in comparing edits, either in small groups or with the whole class. Half a dozen students can be asked to write on the chalkboard and to compare their versions of the same item. (*Note:* In a ghost story, "Something gray and strange passed by in the dim distance" may be better than "A gray rat flapped behind the magnolia across the stream.")

Lesson 52

name:

THE TONE OF A BUSINESS LETTER

Tone is the way writing "sounds" to a reader. Writing often needs editing so that it will sound right. Below is a business letter that needs to be edited for tone. Edit it so that it sounds serious and businesslike. On a separate sheet of paper copy the edited letter.

HINT: A business letter should be clear, factual, and brief. Even if the writer is feeling angry, the tone should not be emotional.

Dear Ms. Silken:

~~I'm very angry, and when I get angry I stay angry.~~ Your company mailed me four Best Cotton T-shirts, at $4.75 each, but you ~~seem~~ charged me for a dozen, that is ~~cool~~ $57½. Please ~~(and if you don't I'm going to sue you; my father is a lawyer)~~ accept my check for $19 in full payment. If there is any difficulty about this, ~~watch out! My spies sometimes~~ *please let me know* ~~get to your part of the country.~~

~~Yours sincerely,~~
~~Affectionately (ha! ha!)~~

Vicia Strongtemp

Extra Write a business letter that needs editing for tone. Give it to a classmate to edit.

page 72   YOU ARE THE EDITOR COPYRIGHT © 1981 I

PURPOSE: To review the proper tone for a business letter and to give practice in editing to create the proper tone (*Answers may vary.*)

This lesson explains itself. Suggest that students not be concerned if their edited version is very short. (*Note:* You may want to discuss whether there is ever a place for fuller, more entertaining writing in business letters. In business, interesting, creatively written letters may be noticed more quickly and may get more action than dull letters.)

PURPOSE: To review choppiness in sentences and to give practice in editing to combine sentences (Answers may vary.)

Go over and discuss the "before" and "after" versions of the two examples. If need be, reinforce these with other examples done on the chalkboard. After students have finished the lesson, discuss the edits, either in groups or with the whole class, or simply read aloud the edit from the answer key and discuss alternatives. Be sure students realize that long, complicated sentences are not always the best sentences. Usually, variety is best.

Lesson 53 name:

COMBINING SENTENCES I

Writing usually sounds best if it contains a variety of sentences—some long and some short. When writing contains too many short, choppy sentences, editors combine them into longer ones. Here are two examples. Read each aloud twice, once as it was before editing, once as edited.

Teaching is a hard job. It is not for lazy people.

The parrot squawked. It flew away. It went into its cage.

Now, edit each of the items below into one sentence. Use the examples above to help you decide how to combine sentences.

1. Mrs. Smith spoiled Jim. Jim was her favorite son.
2. I try to avoid John. The reason is that he has such a bad temper.
3. The house collapsed. It was when the thieves were hiding in it.
4. I don't like peas. However, I eat them to earn my dessert.
5. Skiing can be very risky. Slopes are steep. Snow is slippery.
6. Here is why I admire Jenny. She never does less than her best.
7. The Herbert Nelson School is an excellent school. It's where my grandfather was a pupil. Also, my Aunt Meg taught third grade there.
8. The monkey's mother was killed. The monkey soon died too.

EXTRA Write several items with two or three short, choppy sentences. Edit each item into one sentence. Then give an unedited version to a classmate to edit. Compare the two editings.

PURPOSE: To review choppiness in writing and to give practice in deciding how best to get rid of it without sacrificing sentence variety (Answers may vary.)

Go over the "before" and "after" versions of the example. Deal with any comments or questions. It may be helpful to read the passage aloud so that students will get the meaning of it before they begin editing. Further, it may be well to do the first two lines of the passage together in order to show, for example, how one can argue for and against the comma and *so* after *hungry*. Some will prefer to keep the period and the new sentence here. Read the notes for Lesson 53.

Lesson 54 name:

COMBINING SENTENCES II

The passage below is written with too many short, choppy sentences. Edit it by combining some of the sentences so that it reads more interestingly. You'll need to change some punctuation. For example:

School begins today. and Kevin is happy.

His vacation was boring. There was nothing to do but read. and He also watched TV. He missed all his friends. He missed sports. and He even missed homework. That He was surprised him.

HINT: Read the passage aloud (quietly) to "hear" what needs changing. Change some words, delete some, add some, but don't change the ideas.

When I come home after school I am always hungry so I rush for the refrigerator. Sometimes I don't even see Mom. who She has been waiting. She wants to welcome me. My stomach blinds my eyes. and I hurt her feelings. I shouldn't do this. Really, I'm glad to know Mom cares. One day when I passed her As usual I and went to the fridge. I happened to look around. Mom was laughing. but She was also crying. I was amazed. I went back to Mom's chair. I kissed her on the top of the head. I smiled. and I said, "Hi, Mom!" You should have seen the her expression. It was on her face.

Extra Write a passage in short, jerky sentences. Edit it for sentence variety. Give an unedited copy of the passage to a classmate to edit. Compare the two editings; they will probably be somewhat different.

Lesson 55   name:

SENTENCE VARIETY

Some writers have the problem of stringing too many words and ideas together into a single sentence. Most good writing has a variety of sentences—some long and some short. Editors can help writers create sentence variety. You are the editor. Edit the passage below, which is written as one long, strung-together sentence. You'll need to add and delete words and to change punctuation and capitalization.

First, here's an example of how to do this. Notice carefully how the passage was written before it was edited and what changes the editor made:

Mrs. Jones was an understanding but strict teacher, ~~and~~ she sometimes wrote messages on the chalkboard, ~~and~~ *The* one I remember best was written after recess, ~~because~~ the class had been thoughtless, ~~so~~ *and* the message said, "It's safe to make mistakes in this class, but it's best if you make a different mistake each time," ~~and~~ I've remembered it all my life.

HINT: Editors often read writing aloud to "hear" how it sounds; usually it sounds best with long sentences and short sentences mixed together.

I remember when I first tried to ride a bicycle, ~~because~~ it was a very painful experience, ~~and~~ I was only four years old at the time, so I wasn't very ~~well~~ coordinated, and I had no idea how to balance myself, ~~with the result that I~~ no sooner had climbed on the bike than I was back on the pavement, ~~and~~ I started crying and kept crying louder and louder, ~~and~~ yet I wanted to try it again, *When* I saw my father

PURPOSE: To teach students to "hear" the sound of their sentences and to give practice in editing for achieving variety (*Answers may vary.*)

After students understand the instructions, go over the example carefully and discuss the "before" and "after" versions. Before students start to work on the main passage, make it clear that no one would ever write so "strung-togetherly" as this. The passage is created solely as a challenge to editors. You may want to read the entire passage aloud so that students will get the meaning of it before they start editing.

A good way to correct this lesson is to read aloud the edited version in the answer key, and then to allow students to propose and discuss alternatives. The idea is to learn to hear, to think, and to edit, not to follow a fixed model.

Lesson 55   name:

CONTINUED

walking up the street, coming home from work, ~~and~~ he was always very helpful to me, but he was firm, too, because he felt I should not be spoiled but should learn as much as possible on my own, ~~so~~ he smiled and asked, "Having trouble?" ~~and~~ I sniffled tearfully, "Yeah, I feel awful!" ~~so~~ he told me to get up, pick up my bike, and listen to him, which I did, ~~and~~ then he slowly pushed me along, holding the bike up and showing me how to steer and lean to balance myself, ~~and~~ the first thing I knew he was ten feet behind me, and I was steering and balancing on my own, ~~so~~ I gave a great shout of triumph and immediately crashed again, but it wasn't long before I was riding by myself all over the neighborhood, ~~and~~ I felt very thankful that my father was such a good teacher, ~~and~~ so was my mom thankful, ~~because~~ she liked to have a little peace, which she got now that I was on wheels and falling down only now and then.

EXTRA   Write a passage in one long, strung-together sentence. Edit it for sentence variety, just to be sure it can be done. Then give an unedited copy of the passage to a classmate to edit. Compare the two editings; they will probably be somewhat different.

PURPOSE: To review awkward shifts in the construction of sentences and to give practice in editing such sentences *(Answers may vary.)*

If your students know enough grammar to understand parallel construction, you may wish to explain that parallel construction means that the various grammatical elements in a sentence (or short passage) are similar or comparable; they correspond to each other in tense, construction, number, and so forth. For example, the Caesar sentence goes from simple past to a subordinate clause to a complex form of the past, instead of from one to another of three simple, parallel, past-tense verbs.

To emphasize parallelism, read aloud the suggestions in the answer key, and give students a chance to read aloud and discuss their edits.

RHYTHM AND FLOW
USING PARALLEL CONSTRUCTION

Reading some sentences is like riding on a bumpy road. Here is an example:

"I came and then, when I had seen, I was able to conquer."

That sentence bumps along and doesn't flow well. The word *flow* means to move smoothly from word to word or phrase to phrase or idea to idea. The Roman Emperor Julius Caesar said the same thing:

"I came, I saw, I conquered."

Here's how Caesar might have arrived at his sentence:

I came, ~~and then, when~~ I ^saw^ ~~had seen~~, I ~~was able to~~ conquer^ed^

Caesar's sentence uses *parallel construction*, meaning that each verb in the sentence is in the same form (in this case, the simple past tense): came, saw, conquered (not came, had seen, was able to conquer).

Parallel construction doesn't apply only to verbs. Look at the following sentences. See how the editor has changed them using parallel phrases *(of the people, by the people, for the people):*

Abraham Lincoln favored government of the people, ~~thought it should be~~ by the people, and ~~He wanted it to benefit~~ ^for^ the people.

Edit the following passages using parallel construction so that they flow well. Then on a separate sheet write each in final-draft form.

1. Gravelle ^has^ ~~is the woman with the~~ long blond hair, ~~and who had~~ a chirpy voice, ~~His~~ ^and a^ (face) ~~is also~~ very strong.

2. When Bob saw Verne, she was smiling, ^and^ look^ing^ lively, but ~~also~~ Bob thought she seemed very sad and ~~appeared~~ ^tired.^ ~~to need rest.~~

CONTINUED

3. Playing soccer is fun, ~~to~~ play^ing^ the piano is more fun, and ^playing^ hooky is the most fun of all ~~to be played.~~

4. Because he had never felt a snake, ~~and a reason was~~ ^because^ ~~that~~ he ~~also felt~~ ^was^ scared of animals, and ^because he was^ ~~in addition~~ timid ~~ity was a part of his character,~~ ^so^ he ran away screaming.

5. The children enjoyed it when they messed up the house, ^broke^ ~~breaking~~ toys, play^ed^ loudly when the baby was sleeping, ~~they~~ came home late for supper, and, worst of all, ^told^ lies ~~were told by them.~~

EXTRA Write a passage with good flow and rhythm. Then rewrite it without parallel construction and give that version to a classmate to edit. Compare results.

Lesson 57

name:

CUT WORDINESS

Some writers use too many words. Editors delete needless words to make the writing crisper and more interesting:

One ~~single~~ brave, ~~courageous~~ warrior killed the great ~~big~~ creature ~~dead~~.

Edit the wordiness out of the following passages. (In some cases you may want to delete several needless words and replace them with one new word.)

1. It's a fact, ~~and there's no doubt about it~~ and no one disagrees ~~on the matter~~ that Lance is conceited ~~and stuck-up~~.

2. This ~~is a~~ car ~~which~~ caused a lot of trouble ~~and difficulty~~ the whole ~~entire~~ time Mr. Jones owned ~~and drove~~ it ~~anywhere~~.

3. That is a matter I ~~absolutely~~ refuse to discuss ~~or to talk about~~.

4. Klondike School, ~~which is~~ the finest school ~~for all purposes~~ in the ~~whole~~ region, selects ~~all of~~ its teachers with care, *and* ~~It is a fine school also because it~~ pays them well, ~~which is a good thing~~.

5. ~~It~~ is nice that he can take a joke ~~on himself at his own expense, and that is~~ one ~~real~~ reason that I admire him.

6. The farmer planted seeds, ~~in the ground under the dirt,~~ then watered them every day ~~with water~~ until they sprouted ~~up out of the earth~~.

Extra Write several passages that have extra, needless words and give them to a classmate to edit.

page 79   YOU ARE THE EDITOR COPYRIGHT © 1981

PURPOSE: To increase students' awareness of needless words and to give practice in editing them out (*Answers may vary.*)

Go over the "before" and "after" versions of the example and discuss them. After that, the lesson is fairly straightforward. (*Note:* It's only fair to recognize that many people, sad to say, are impressed by wordiness. A skilled writer may have to allow for this fact and may be wordier than would otherwise be desirable. This would be a good time to discuss, also, whether it is ever justifiable to pad a paper just to make it come out with the number of words required by an assignment.)

Lesson 58

name:

FORMAL AND INFORMAL WRITING

The characters above are reacting *informally* and *formally* to a ball breaking the window. Writing, too, can be formal or informal. In formal writing you choose your words to sound serious and respectful, and you don't use slang. Informal writing may use slang and other words and phrases to sound friendly and relaxed. You'd write a formal letter to the Queen of England. You'd write an informal note to your best friend.

The first five sentences below are informal writing. Edit them into formal writing. The next three are formal. Edit them into informal writing. Sentences 1 and 6 have been done for you.

INFORMAL REACTION   FORMAL REACTION

Informal to Formal

1. *We must leave* ~~Let's scram~~ before we *are arrested* ~~get pinched~~ by the *police* ~~cops~~.
2. My *mother never stopped bothering me* ~~mom bugged me no end~~ about my *bad friends* ~~no-good pals~~.
3. That *student truly enjoys* ~~cat is really into~~ books *more than televisions* ~~instead of the tubes~~.
4. George *retires* ~~hits the sack~~ early so he can get *a great deal of sleep* ~~plenty of shut-eye~~.
5. Mayella *greatly dislikes* ~~just can't stand~~ people who *talk* ~~keep yakking~~ all day long instead of *earning a living* ~~picking up a few bucks~~.

Formal to Informal
(Look up unfamiliar words in the dictionary.)

6. *Bob* ~~Robert~~ will *ask* ~~request~~ Ann to *leave right now* ~~make her departure immediately~~.
7. At the Smith *'s* ~~residence,~~ *they eat* dinner ~~is served precisely~~ at 6:30 *on the dot*.
8. *Getting along with* ~~Relating to~~ others *means you've got to try hard to see it* ~~requires a maximum effort to understand~~ their *way* ~~circumstances~~.

EXTRA Write two formal sentences, and edit them into informal English. Then write two informal sentences and edit them into formal English. Now give your unedited sentences to a classmate to edit. Compare results.

page 80   YOU ARE THE EDITOR COPYRIGHT © 1981

PURPOSE: To review formal and informal writing and to give practice in editing from one tone to the other (*Answers may vary.*)

Explain that neither formal nor informal prose is better—the use of either depends on the purpose and on the audience. Go over the "before" and "after" versions of passage 1. Discuss in small groups and with the whole class the results of the edit. You may want to reinforce the results by having a student extemporaneously speak a formal sentence and another speak the same idea informally, and vice versa. Point out that there are not only various levels of formality (from extremely stiff, highfalutin, and stilted to just plain serious), but also various levels of informality (from casual and familiar to slang). These are subtle matters, subject to judgment, and the object is to develop awareness of tone.

PURPOSE: **To review the need for both developing and cutting various parts of a passage to increase interest and to give practice in editing these two problems** (*Answers may vary.*)

Point out that certain passages have both yawn-producing sections and tell-me-more sections and that editors should be aware of both. Can students remember examples of both in writing done in class this year? This lesson can be done rather quickly; thus, encourage students who finish early to start on the *Extra*. Discuss the recommended "cuts" and "devs" and also point out where new paragraphs are needed.

DEVELOP INTEREST AND CUT DULLNESS

Editors remind writers to cut out what is boring or useless in their writing. Editors also remind writers to develop the more interesting parts. To *develop* means to "add more facts and details."

In the following passage several things need to be cut out. Other things need to be developed. Edit the passage by underlining once what should be developed. Then write *dev* in the margin. Underline twice what should be cut and write *cut* in the margin. Also show where new paragraphs should begin. One *cut* and one *dev* have been done to show to how.

cut	That morning I got up at 8:00, about thirty minutes later than usual, <u>because I usually get up at
dev	7:30.</u> I had a delicious breakfast. <u>Then I hurried down
dev	the steps, fell, and hurt myself.</u> Later, all confused, <u>I
dev	saw a guy leaning against a doorway. He spoke to me
dev	and pulled a knife. I gave him my money.</u> Then I went
	on toward school thinking what I would tell my
cut	friends <u>whose names are Susan, Doris, Abbie, Mike, Leo,
cut	and one whose name I can't spell.</u> I was so worried
dev	that <u>I almost got run over by a bus, and the driver
dev	swore at me. I didn't bleed much when I banged into
dev/cut	the lamppost.</u> I now had four streets to cross to get to
cut	school, <u>Arch Street, Vine Street, Race Street, and Main
cut/dev	Street.</u> When I finally got to school, <u>everybody looked at
dev	me, asked me questions, and even insulted me.</u>

EXTRA Write a similar passage for a classmate to edit. OR: Rewrite part or all of the passage above, cutting and developing as you think best. Make up the specific details you need.

PURPOSE: **To give practice in proofreading, using editor's marks for corrections, as a review and/or a test**

This lesson requires exactness, and there is only one correct set of answers. Turn students loose on it in class or at home. If done in class, it can serve as a gradable test of proofreading skill. (You should probably tell students in advance whether or not you are going to grade the lesson.)

PROOFREAD FOR CARELESS ERRORS

The last step in editing is *proofreading*. Proofreading involves looking over a paper and correcting any mistakes that are left, no matter how small.

Proofread the passage below. The content does not need changing. However, there are more than sixty mistakes you'll need to fix with editor's marks. When you've finished, copy the passage on a separate sheet of paper and proofread your copy.

Helping an Ol Man in Trouble

One Saturdy morning some Cub Scout were late to theirs den meeting. The den mother asked, "Wy are you so late?"

"Oh," said a bight small boy, "we wer helping an old man cross the steet."

"That's very kind," said the den mother, "but that shouldn't make you half an hour late. Why are you so lat."

The boys look at each other with much embarrassment. The bright boy poked an larger boy who looked brave. He smiled at the floor and then at the den mother. "Well," he said, "the old man didn't want want to go."

Extra Write a paper very clearly. Then add a number of careless errors. Have a classmate proofread and correct it.

Lesson 61

name:

EDIT FOR STYLE: A REVIEW

The passage below is an editorial to be published in a school newspaper. It will be read by students, teachers, and parents. It needs editing badly. You are the editor, and your job is to edit for *style* so that the writing will be suitable for its readers. For example, you would edit out phrases such as "Gee whiz!" or "That's neat-o!" However, do not cut out or add any ideas. Mark two or three places that should be developed (write *dev* in the margin). There are about a dozen wordy places to shorten, two or three sentences to cut out, and several words that need replacing. Also, paragraphing is needed. There are no spelling or punctuation errors in the passage.

The first three sentences have been done for you. Also the first *dev* is marked. Since different editors will edit differently, use your own best judgment. (Look up unfamiliar words in the dictionary.)

Honesty or ~~Crooks and Liars~~ Dishonesty in the Seventh Grade?

It's hard to tell the truth, hard to resist cheating, and hard not to steal, but dishonesty has ~~proceeded excessively~~ gone too far in our seventh grade. ~~Man, I really mean it!~~ Hardly ~~seven days~~ a week or even ~~twenty-four hours~~ a day passes without ~~that~~ some ~~skunk does~~ student doing a dishonest act. Let me prove it. Over half the ~~kids~~ students in the class said that ~~stuff of theirs~~ their possessions had been ~~snitched~~ stolen during the month of February 1980. Remember the

dev example of the evil theft that happened? And

dev absolutely nobody ever tells the ~~veracity when it comes~~ truth

dev ~~to what concerns work done at~~ about home work. People are

better at ~~false~~ excuses than ~~true~~ work. ¶ What can we

do about ~~the nefarious~~ this trouble situation? ~~that faces us all?~~

dev First, we must follow the guidelines. ~~I mean the~~

dev ~~guidelines~~ of the student-teacher committee. ~~This is~~

PURPOSE: To review and test students' skill in editing for style *(Answers may vary.)*

Students of lesser ability can respond to parts of this lesson; the lesson will also challenge the very able students. You may want to read the entire passage aloud so that students will get the meaning of it before they start editing. Be sure the directions are well understood, and examine carefully the three sentences already edited and the one passage marked for development. Deal with any questions. When the lesson is finished, read and discuss several different edits. This lesson can also be used as a test if you want to collect and mark the papers, using your best judgment as to how well each student has succeeded. You may want to underline any passage that you think is misedited and put in the margin whichever of the symbols teachers use (listed on page 100 in the "Writer/Editor's Handbook") that is most appropriate.

Lesson 61

name:

CONTINUED

dev ~~the committee~~ that met. ~~It met~~ last week. Second,

each ~~individual, single~~ person should promise ~~three~~ make three

~~newly established kinds of behavior,~~ ~~to tell the truth,~~ never to lie,

never to steal, and ~~not to~~ ~~be dishonest~~ never to cheat. ~~It is my~~

¶ I think ~~genuine opinion~~ that honesty can become a habit—

if we work on it and if we encourage each other.

The good habit can drive out the bad. ~~We must do~~

~~it.~~ Otherwise, ~~our class has~~ we will have a sad future. ~~I mean~~

~~a sad future~~ as a class and as individuals. ~~Wow!~~

~~Come on, kids, let's go!~~

EXTRA Make up details and develop the spots you marked *dev.* Then copy the editorial as a final draft and proofread it. OR: Write a passage that needs editing for style and give it to a classmate to edit.

PURPOSE: To test, in an objective manner, the student's knowledge of editor's marks

Although this test has not been standardized on any broad sampling, it is reasonable to require a perfect score as a passing mark: Either you know the uses of the editor's marks or you don't. Thus, to get a check in the first square of the Editor's Certificate (page 90), a student must score sixteen. You may give the test as often as necessary for students to achieve perfect scores.

name: _____

TEST I: DO YOU KNOW YOUR EDITOR'S MARKS?

Directions: In the left column there are sixteen statements. Each tells what a certain editor's mark does. In the two right columns there are three editor's marks for each numbered statement. Decide which is the correct mark for each statement and circle A, B, or C. Try this sample:

0. Use a capital letter.   0. A   (B)   C

The correct answer is B. Circle the B.

1. Put a period here.
2. Add something here.
3. Start a new paragraph here.
4. Transpose letters or words.
5. Delete or remove something.
6. Put an apostrophe here.
7. Change a letter.
8. Use a capital letter.
9. Put a quotation mark here.
10. Close the gap.
11. Keep the deleted material.
12. Run lines together; no paragraph.
13. Remove the item and close the gap.
14. Make a space here.
15. Use a comma here.
16. Use a small letter.

PURPOSE: To test, in an objective manner, the student's ability to recognize the needed editing in a passage and to use editor's marks to do the editing

There are thirty-six items in this test. Read aloud the instruction page and answer all questions about it.

Score the tests and make a distribution of scores to find the median (middle, *not* average) score. Students may be interested in knowing how they scored in comparison to the median. Our judgment is that any score of thirty or above rates a check in the second box on the Editor's Certificate (page 90) even if the median is above that score. Those who score below thirty may continue to take the test until they reach an acceptable score. (With each retake the score for awarding the certificate might be one point higher.)

Note: Emphasize that the main purpose of both Tests I and II is to learn editing, not to earn a certificate, but that with careful review and further study most students will be able to earn their certificates.

name: _____

TEST II ANSWER SHEET

Circle one letter for each item.

1. A   The Auto repair
   B   The Auto repair
   C   The Auto repair

2. A   me and Mom
   B   me and Mom
   C   me and Mom

3. A   always some crummy
   B   always some crummy
   C   always some crummy

4. A   troubles a stuck
   B   troubles a stuck
   C   troubles a stuck

5. A   a rattle a cieling
   B   a rattle a cieling
   C   a rattle a cieling

6. A   early on saturday
   B   early on saturday
   C   early on saterday

7. A   there always some people
   B   there always some people
   C   there's always some people

8. A   hear, I ex-
   B   hear, I ex-
   C   hear, I ex-

9. A   wait. At last we
   B   wait. At last we
   C   wait. At last we

10. A   I investigate him. "No,
    B   I investigate him. "No,
    C   I investigate him. "No,

11. A   the dope, looks
    B   the dope protests, looks
    C   the dope protests looks

12. A   he shouts, the 2nd action
    B   he shouts, the 2nd action
    C   he shouts the 2nd action

13. A   sat down, and try
    B   sat down, and try
    C   sat down, and try

14. A   tires, stupid grinding noises,
    B   tires, stupid grinding noises,
    C   tires, stupid grinding noises,

15. A   and so forth That
    B   and so forth That
    C   and so forth. That

16. A   Also I cant con centrate
    B   Also I cant con centrate
    C   Also I cant con centrate

name: _____

17. A pretty inpatient, and tell
    B pretty inpatient, and tell
    C pretty inpatient, and tell

18. A doesn't seem to here. Now
    B doesn't seem to hear. Now
    C doesn't seem to hear. Now

19. A them with its hood open.
    B them with their hood open.
    C them with their hood open.

20. A are eating the heds
    B eats the heds
    C is eating the heds

21. A noises there, and!
    B noises there, are!
    C noises there are.

22. A snake invisible to me hisses.
    B snake invisible to me, I hisses.
    C snake invisible to I, hisses.

23. A perambulating over to them
    B perambulating over to them
    C walking over to them it

24. A You want get to hurt."
    B You want get to hurt."
    C You want get to hurt."

25. A room. All most getting
    B room. All most getting
    C room. All most getting

26. A slots. Act four are
    B slots. Act four are
    C slots. Act four are

27. A another hour. When a
    B another hour. When a
    C another hour. When a

28. A "How did we do, she states?"
    B "How did we do, she asks?"
    C "How did we do, she states?"

29. A he says, "every things
    B he says, "every things
    C he said, "every things

30. A started over to the cashiers
    B started over to the cashiers
    C started over to the cashiers

31. A stat that some trouble."
    B that some trouble."
    C stat that some trouble."

32. A counter, and lifted
    B counter. And lifted
    C counter, and lifted

33. A embarrassment. Oh, gee,"
    B embarrassment, Oh gee,"
    C embarrassment, Oh gee,"

34. A "Well, remove it away,
    B "Well, take it away,
    C "Well, remove it away,

35. A he added, "we dont
    B he added, "we dont
    C he added, "we dont

36. A wagons." THE END!
    B wagons." THE END!
    C wagons." THE END!

ABOUT THE AUTHOR

Eric W. Johnson has taught English and social studies for more than twenty-five years in grades 5 through 12 in public and private schools. At present he advises teachers and administrators on methods of teaching, on curriculum, and on relationships between home and school, as well as leading workshops on the teaching of writing. He is the author of twenty-seven books, among which are *How to Achieve Competence in English*, *How to Live Through Junior High School*, *Improve Your Own Spelling*, *Life into Language*, *Our World into Words*, *Stories in Perspective*, and *Teaching School: Points Picked Up*. He is a co-author of *Adventures for You*, *Four Famous Adventures*, and *Language for Daily Use*. Mr. Johnson is a graduate of Germantown Friends School, Harvard College, and the Harvard Graduate School of Education. He is married, lives in Philadelphia, and he and his wife have three grown children.